PENGUIN BOOKS

LITERARY AGENTS

Adam Begley, a freelance journalist and critic, is a frequent contributor to *The New York Times Magazine* and a contributing editor at *The Paris Review* and *Lingua Franca*. For two years he wrote about publishing for New York City newspapers, and for another two years wrote a monthly books column for *Mirabella*. He lives in Wisconsin.

LITERARY

AGENTS

A Writer's Guide

ADAM BEGLEY

PENGUIN BOOKS

PENGUIN BOOKS
Published by the Penguin Group
Penguin Books USA Inc., 375 Hudson Street,
New York, New York 10014, U.S.A.
Penguin Books Ltd, 27 Wrights Lane,
London W8 5TZ, England
Penguin Books Australia Ltd, Ringwood,
Victoria, Australia
Penguin Books Canada Ltd, 10 Alcorn Avenue,
Toronto, Ontario, Canada M4V 3B2
Penguin Books (N.Z.) Ltd, 182–190 Wairau Road,
Auckland 10, New Zealand

Penguin Books Ltd, Registered Offices:
Harmondsworth, Middlesex, England

First published in the United States of America by Poets & Writers, Inc.,
1978
Revised edition published 1983
Second revised edition published 1988
This third revised edition published in Penguin Books 1993

5 7 9 10 8 6

Copyright © Poets & Writers, Inc., 1993
All rights reserved

LIBRARY OF CONGRESS CATALOGING IN PUBLICATION DATA
Begley, Adam.
Literary agents: a writer's guide/ Adam Begley.—Rev. 4th ed.
p. cm.
Rev. ed. of: Literary agents/ Debby Mayer. 1988.
Includes bibliographical references.
ISBN 0 14 01.7215 7
1. Literary agents. I. Mayer, Debby. Literary agents.
II. Title.
PN163.B44   1993
070.5'2—dc20   92–32475

Printed in the United States of America
Set in Times Roman
Designed by Debbie Glasserman

CONTENTS

INTRODUCTION

Poets & Writers, Inc., is pleased to present the completely revised fourth edition of *Literary Agents: A Writer's Guide,* written by Adam Begley and published by Penguin Books.

Since 1970 Poets & Writers has been the central source of practical information for writers in the United States. Writers are solitary workers, and the services of Poets & Writers help fill their need for community, communication, and professional information.

Poets & Writers staff members meet writers at conferences and seminars throughout the country. And the Information Center at Poets & Writers answers almost ten thousand questions each year on such practical subjects as writing workshops and conferences, resources and reference guides, and literary agents. Questions about how to find and work with a literary agent run second only to queries about how to get published, and the two often come together, representing between them about a third of all questions received.

The first chapter of this book answers the first two questions writers most often have about agents:

- What exactly does a literary agent do?
- How much does an agent charge?

How to find an agent and the terms of the writer-agent agreement are covered in chapters Two and Three. In Chapter Four, established agents and authors talk about the business. The last two chapters explain the advantages and disadvantages of "nontraditional" agents; they are followed by lists of agents and places to find additional help.

Writing is an art and a profession that brings immense satisfaction; it's also a business that can be difficult and extremely frustrating, a business in which writers are ultimately responsible for themselves and their manuscripts. Though the written work is completed, the writer's work is still unfinished. We at Poets & Writers are proud to add this book to the services and publications we offer as a guide to the business of writing.

The lists of agents at the back of this book could not have been completed without the help of Jim Andrews and Nori Negron of the Poets & Writers staff. Many thanks to them for fact-checking and data entry.

Debby Mayer
Publications Director
Poets & Writers, Inc.

LITERARY AGENTS

CHAPTER ONE

THE LITERARY AGENT: WHO NEEDS ONE AND WHY?

If a book appears in bookstores bearing the imprint of a major publisher, the chances are excellent that the author is represented by a literary agent. Any writer with a publishable manuscript or a viable proposal will try to hire the services of an agent. Most well-known and commercially successful authors who can pick and choose among competing publishers use an agent as a buffer to distance themselves from the messy details of negotiations and contracts and royalty statements. The agent takes care of the business; the writer sticks to writing.

Some authors come to rely on their agents for literary advice, others for stability. In theory, a writer need only go through the process of finding an agent once, whereas each new book usually requires a new contract, sometimes a new editor, or even a new publisher. Editors change houses, often without warning; publishing companies go out of business, merge with other houses, or redefine themselves entirely. Faced with these uncertainties, the writer looks to an agent for continuity.

Just because it's "standard practice," however, doesn't mean that all writers have an agent, or that all writers even need an agent. John Updike doesn't have one; neither does Stephen King. Some writers fall into a relationship with a particular house and never feel the need for an intermediary; others make a conscious choice to deal directly with their publishers.

Stephen Dixon, whose novel *Frog* was nominated for a 1991 National Book Award, has published fourteen books, none of them with the assistance of an agent. Of some 350 short stories he's had published, only two were placed, several years ago, by an agent. Over the years Dixon has decided that he doesn't *want* an agent. "I love the idea of not having an intermediary between me and my editors," he says. Furthermore, he declares himself content with small advances. For writers less indifferent to the financial rewards of the literary life, agents can often assume an enormous importance, seemingly the sole means to a lucrative end.

In some extreme cases, however—brand-name authors and starving poets for example—agents can be less than useful or prohibitively expensive. For a writer who can confidently expect generous offers from many publishers for each book he or she writes, a lawyer with publishing expertise who bills his or her clients at an hourly rate might make more sense than an agent who charges a 15-percent commission (see Chapter Five). Only rarely will an agent even agree to represent a writer who doesn't make money and isn't ever likely to, and this excludes most poets and many short-story writers. There is relatively little negotiation involved in selling a poem or a short story to a small magazine or shoestring press, and the income from such sales, while precious to the writer, is rarely enough to interest an agent. (Of 233 agents surveyed in this book, only 23 said they would consider taking on a prospective client who sent in a collection of poems.)

Hopeful first-time authors often send their work directly to publishing houses for the simple reason that they can't convince an agent to represent them—it can be nearly as difficult for an unknown writer to find an agent as to find an editor at an appropriate publishing house. And yet many publishers neglect, ignore, or flatly reject manuscripts that are not submitted by agents. This is the widely recognized and much lamented double bind that welcomes the newcomer to the curious world of book publishing.

In the end, "standard practice" seems most sensible: a writer who has in hand a marketable property—that is, a book-length work or a proposal for a book-length work—should consider hiring an agent. This advice is offered to first-time authors and battle-scarred veterans alike; it covers books already in print as well as manuscripts fresh from the typewriter (a writer can decide that he or she needs to be represented by an agent at any point in the publishing process). But advice should always come weighted with a caveat, and in this case there are two: a bad agent can be worse than no agent, and all agents, even the most effective, are at best a necessary evil. In the best of all possible worlds, writers and publishers would work in concert, with no need for a middleman. But nearly all publishing companies are concerned first and foremost with their own profit margins. Authors generally have other things in mind, whether they are marketing possibilities or literary excellence. Agents try to bridge the gap between the author's hopes and the reality offered by the publisher.

WHAT DOES A LITERARY AGENT DO?

A good agent promotes and protects the writer's interests by finding a suitable editor at a suitable publishing house, negotiating a favorable contract, watching over the publishing process, collecting all payments due, and keeping accurate records. The best agents also plan for the future; they advise their authors on how to manage a successful career. Thus an effective agent becomes the author's sales representative, business manager, and consultant.

Sometimes this relationship grows into close friendship. A recent book about Eudora Welty and her agent, Diarmuid Russell, tells the story of an extraordinary literary partnership marked by deep affection and loyalty. But at the outset, writer and agent meet on professional ground. Here are some of the things an agent can do for a writer.

The Hunt for an Editor

Few writers are familiar with more than a handful of editors; most know the names of a half dozen prominent publishing houses, and that's it. The agent, however, is presumed to be reasonably well acquainted not only with a wide range of publishers, from tiny independent presses to multinational conglomerates, but also with the key editors at each establishment. The agent can put this knowledge to use in the following ways:

- Formulating a sales pitch. The agent should have a general plan for how to sell the writer's work and also know how to tailor the presentation to fit the taste of individual editors.
- Submitting only to appropriate houses. This means avoiding unstable publishing companies as well as those with a history of poor performance with the kind of book on offer.
- Making sure the project receives due consideration. An agent with a good reputation should have some clout and extensive personal contacts.
- Matching the writer with the right editor. Just because an editor shows interest in a particular project doesn't mean the editor and the writer will work well together.
- Sending out multiple submissions. When a proposal or manuscript is mailed to several publishers at once, the whole process moves faster (agents do this routinely, but publishers sometimes disapprove of writers who try it themselves).

- Finding foreign publishers, usually with the help of foreign-based subagents (see page 11).

Getting to Yes

For some writers, an agent's most important function is negotiating the contract, and the important part of the negotiation is the dollar amount of the advance. Anyone who has struggled to earn a living as a writer will understand this itch to quickly earn large sums of money. But a good agent is thinking about much more than the size of the first payment.

To the layman, the contracts issued by publishing houses are complicated documents even in their basic "boilerplate" form. Agents usually seek to make changes in these contracts or add clauses beneficial to the writer. When the legal and financial intricacies have all been hammered out, the agent should be able to present the writer with an agreement suited to his or her needs. An agent may try to arrange the best possible deal by doing any of the following:

- Conducting an auction to obtain a larger advance or more favorable terms. Auctions are appropriate only to projects with broad appeal and good commercial prospects; moreover, the book must be suited to a number of different houses.
- Retaining certain subsidiary rights. Publishers want to buy as many rights as possible, and in some cases the writer does well to sell them. The publisher, however, is not always in the business of making

money for the writer, so a writer's interests may be better served if the agent can manage to curb the publisher's acquisitive instinct and keep some rights for the writer (see "Rights for Sale," page 27).

- Arranging a schedule of payments that meets the author's immediate and long-term needs. Some well-paid writers prefer to receive their advance in regular installments rather than wait for lump sums on uncertain dates fixed by convention, such as on delivery of the completed manuscript or on the publication date.

- Requesting contract clauses that stipulate certain conditions. For example, a minimum advertising and promotion budget, a minimum first printing, or authorial control over jacket design (publishers don't often accept these kinds of conditions, but on the other hand agents don't often insist).

- Adding bonus clauses tied to the book's performance, including number of copies shipped, appearance(s) on the best-seller list, the release of a movie or appearance of a television version.

The Follow-Through

The popular image of the agent wheeling and dealing, always in the thick of the action, is the product of a basic misconception. The spotlight is on when an agent strikes a lucrative deal: the media descend, report on the stunning coup, and vanish. But most of the work, much of it dull routine, goes on before and, especially, after the contract has been negotiated, and many good, solid deals don't make headlines. As long as the book is in print, and as long as there is any interest (or the prospect of any interest) in the rights attached to it, the agent should be on the job. In the months and years after a contract is signed, the agent's less glamorous duties include

- Resolving any conflicts between author and editor or author and publisher.
- Monitoring the publishing process to ensure that the terms of the contract are fulfilled.
- Obtaining prompt royalty statements, verifying their accuracy, and, if possible, explaining them to the author (there are few documents more impenetrable to the uninitiated than a publisher's royalty statement).
- Collecting all payments due the author. The money a book earns under contracts negotiated by the agent is generally sent directly to the agent, who then deducts the agency commission, plus expenses, before passing payment on to the author (this arrangement persists as long as the contracts are in force, even if author and agent part company).
- Selling any rights not already sold to the publisher.
- Recording printing histories and sales records.
- Handling mail sent to the author care of the agent.

Taking the Long View

Of the many ways in which an agent can foster a writer's career, giving sound advice can be the most important.

Not all agents are equally well equipped for dispensing wisdom, and yet almost every agent knows enough to weigh today's choices against tomorrow's prospects. It's especially important that young writers develop a sense of how to build an audience, how to forge a lasting connection with a publisher, and how to respond to media attention. Even established authors can benefit from a shrewd analysis of the current publishing climate.

There's no standard prescription for what kind of counsel an agent should provide, and this is certainly not the kind of service that can be outlined in any formal agreement between an author and his or her agent. However, an agent may help to shape a writer's future by

- Suggesting changes to a proposal or a manuscript. Publishers are less and less likely these days to accept material that they feel will require substantial revision, and so agents sometimes act as editors to make sure that submitted work has found its finished form.
- Introducing a writer who is "between books" to an editor who has a project in mind (the books that result from this kind of matchmaking are almost always nonfiction).
- Offering to submit the writer's work to low- or nonpaying prestige publications.
- Discouraging ill-conceived projects.

HOW MUCH DO AGENTS CHARGE?

Almost all literary agents work on a commission basis; they usually take either 10 or 15 percent of an author's domestic earnings. A decade ago, 10-percent commissions were standard, but the lower rate is now increasingly rare.

To gather information for this book, Poets & Writers surveyed the 472 literary agencies listed in the 1991 *Literary Market Place*. Of the 240 agencies that responded, 233 agreed to be listed. Of those, 173 charge a 15-percent commission, and 45 charge 10 percent; 15 declined to disclose their commission. Many agents continue to offer their longtime clients the lower rate and charge newcomers more; some agents will fix the commission according to the writer's publishing history (a first-time author will have to pay the higher rate).

It's difficult to tell a writer to disregard the commission rate when choosing an agent—after all, there's a 50-percent difference between the low and high ends of the scale. But experience suggests that the rate of commission almost never determines the success of an author-agent relationship. There are agents who ask for a 15-percent commission and then go out and double the writer's income; on the other hand, there are 10-percent agents who do very little to earn their keep.

As mentioned earlier, payments due the author are almost always sent directly to the agent, who deducts his or her commission before passing the money on.

When selling foreign rights, the agent usually works with subagents based abroad. Subagents perform in other countries most of the same tasks that the principal agent performs at home: they look for the right editor at the right house, negotiate a contract, monitor the publishing process, and collect the advance, the royalties, and any other payments due. The subagent deducts a commission (almost always 10 percent) and sends the balance to the principal agent, who also takes a cut. The two commissions on foreign sales usually add up to 20 percent.

Many agencies also deduct certain expenses from the writer's earnings. These may include

- photocopying costs
- registration and insurance of mail
- telegrams, faxes, and long-distance telephone calls
- messenger service (the publishing industry makes extensive use of New York's bicycle messengers, and somebody has to pay for them)

Because agencies make their money from commissions, they can seldom afford to represent writers whose work they think can't be sold. If an author earns on the average less than five thousand dollars a year from writing, the commissions won't be sufficient to interest most agents. There are, however, exceptions to this rule. Young writers sometimes find agents willing to bet on their future, and some agents represent authors in whose work, though it has no commercial appeal, they have a passionate belief. Agents know as well as writers that a book's literary merit very often has little or nothing to do with its chances for popular success. And just as there are publishers who take on prestigious authors whose books sell poorly, so, too, there are agents eager to have respected writers on their list whether or not they generate income.

But if years go by and the agent spends valuable time pitching manuscripts that are repeatedly rejected or sell for tiny sums, the writer, sad to say, will eventually be rejected, too.

CHAPTER TWO

HOW DOES A WRITER
FIND AN AGENT?

A list of the names and addresses of 196 literary agents who do not charge reading fees begins on page 63 of this book. Staring at the agents' names, however, won't help a hopeful author pick the right one.

Establishing certain broad parameters can help the bewildered writer make a better choice. Some may decide, for instance, to consider only large, New York–based agencies; writers who live far from New York may want an agent closer to home; and some may ignore geography entirely and seek out personalized attention from a tiny agency located almost anywhere, even on another continent. This kind of decision is somewhat arbitrary: a small, well-run agency can provide better, and as varied, service, as a large, poorly run agency; and though New York agencies will always claim to have the ear of the publishing industry, the fax machine has made agenting from any corner of the world perfectly feasible.

The easy way to choose is to ask for a recommendation from a friendly fellow writer, teacher, or editor. But the recommendation must cut both ways: the writer is looking for an agent worth hiring, and the agent wants to know that the writer's work is worth reading. If both conditions are met, and agent and author get along at once, the search is over. Sadly, the process is rarely that simple. Prominent agents are overwhelmed by solicitations from eager writers; their attention is hard to catch, their skepticism hard to conquer.

FINDING A WILLING AGENT

For the unknown writer, any personal recommendation helps. The best source is a book editor who has expressed serious interest in the writer's work, in part because that editor's interest will be taken as a sign of the material's commercial viability. Many editors try to maintain a purely literary relationship with their authors; they like to keep their editing tasks separate from the business aspects of acquiring a manuscript, and they prefer to negotiate a contract with the author's agent. Editors who are already interested in a writer's work are therefore often happy to furnish a short list of suitable agents.

Writing teachers are likely to know of a number of different agents. A distinguished teacher's recommendation carries weight but isn't guaranteed to convince a busy agent. Magazine editors may also be willing to help.

Established agents say that most of their new clients are referred to them by other writers they've represented. The enthusiastic recommendation of a fellow writer is indeed an excellent calling card. Writers are often familiar only with their own agents, however, and in many cases only a writer's own agent will be swayed by a recommendation.

A writer without contacts, who has no opportunity to ask for a recommendation (or who has asked without success), will have to choose prospective agents more or less at random, approach them "cold"—that is, without prior introduction—and convince them to take on a new client.

In the acknowledgments at the beginning of many books—even novels—the author thanks his or her agent. By leafing through the hardcovers at a local bookstore, writers can easily compile a list of agents who represent works at least roughly similar to their own (and these are agents with apparently grateful clients). The next step is to get a foot in the door.

Unsolicited manuscripts, no matter how persuasive the cover letter, are automatically rejected by most agencies (and by many publishers). The writer must rely instead on the artful query—a hybrid communication that's part cover letter, part proposal, part self-promotion.

A few agents will consider a query only if it is accompanied by a credible recommendation. But of the

240 agents who responded to the Poets & Writers survey, 227 indicated that they would read queries sent cold through the mail. (A query that arrives without a self-addressed, stamped envelope for reply will almost always be ignored. Most agents discourage phone queries and the faxing of queries as well.)

There are as many ways to write a query as there are to write a love letter, but one feature is essential: a concise, evocative description of the work to be marketed. An outline is helpful, and a *short* sample. Biographical information is also important. Publications should be listed in full, including small magazines, newsletters, or alternative newspapers.

There's no reason not to send out several queries at once, as long as the agents are informed. If there's been no reply to a query after three weeks, it's time to telephone and ask, politely, for a response. (Agents say they pay attention to the manners of the writers who contact them; they avoid the discourteous on the grounds that those individuals will likely be difficult to work with.)

If more than one agent expresses interest and asks to see another sample or an entire manuscript, the fortunate writer is nonetheless in a bind: many agents will only read "on exclusive." That is, they don't want to spend time on work that's also being looked at by their competitors. Yet showing the material to one agent at a time can take months.

Poets & Writers suggests the following compromise procedure: the agents should be granted a limited exclusivity. The first-choice agent gets the manuscript and is allowed ten working days in which to give an initial response (not a firm commitment). If the ten days go by and there's no answer, the second-choice agent (who has also seen a sample and responded to a query) gets a copy of the manuscript with the same condition attached. It should be made clear that giving the manuscript to the second agent does not mean that it's being withdrawn from the first, and so on. This system requires some tact on the part of the writer (it's not a good idea to let an agent know that he or she is anything but first choice); it's also fair and relatively efficient. Some agents won't go along with the scheme, but most will.

If no agent expresses interest after a first round of queries, subsequent rounds are certainly in order. Persistence pays in this kind of endeavor: 472 agents were listed in the 1991 *Literary Market Place,* and each of them had a different idea of what was marketable.

If, after looking for some time, a writer finds only one willing agent, the temptation to give up and take what's offered should be resisted. Most agents will accept without quibble the idea that a writer needs some time before making a firm commitment—two weeks, say. That time can be profitably spent following up on queries still pending and even contacting a few new agents. With a solid offer in hand, the writer will find this last quick round of queries surprisingly painless.

A writer suffering any real qualms about signing with a particular agent should express his or her doubts in a forthright manner and suggest that looking around for a while longer might dispel those doubts. An agent who reacts violently to the news that a prospective client is having second thoughts may very well be in the wrong business.

The writer who *chooses* his or her agent generally approaches the relationship with a constructive and co-operative attitude. The writer who feels stuck with the only agent who would bite makes for a less willing partner. Agents know this. Writers should be tactful and considerate about shopping around, but they should also keep in mind that in the end the agent will be happy to have been chosen.

CHOOSING AMONG WILLING AGENTS

A herd instinct motivates much of what happens in the publishing industry, and so an author with a particularly appealing manuscript or proposal may find many agents to choose from. More and more frequently in recent years, authors who receive this kind of flattering attention have been conducting formal interviews with a short list of prospective agents.

An agent who's been in business for a number of years builds a list of clients and develops a reputation among authors and editors. Listening to word of mouth, therefore, is one dependable approach to the problem of choosing an agent. But for any writer, and especially those who mistrust the industry buzz or are too far removed from publishing circles to hear it at all, there's really no substitute for direct contact of some sort with the interested agents—a long telephone call or an exchange of letters at the very least.

There are agents who will provide a complete list of their clients only to acquisitions editors in publishing houses, but even the most discreet agents will tell a prospective client what kind of writers they represent and offer to name a few by way of example. If the names provided by the agent are obscure, the writer may want to do some research. Are these reputable authors? Are the books well published? Armed with some ideas about the clients on the agent's list and a first-hand glimpse of the agent's personal style, the writer is left to make a sensitive decision that will always be based at least in part on instinct.

"I'LL TAKE BOTH"

Every now and then a clever writer decides that two agents are better than one and schemes to hire one agent for one set of rights and another for the rest. Very few agents will accept this kind of piecemeal arrangement. An agent who agrees to represent an author usually expects to take on whatever that author writes, not just one manuscript, and to handle all the associated rights for each book. Screenwriting is an exception to this rule: writers who moonlight for the movies almost always seek out a Hollywood agent in addition to their literary agent.

For most writers, one agent is plenty.

CHAPTER THREE

THE AUTHOR-AGENT RELATIONSHIP

Mutual trust and confidence keep writer and agent working together happily. The writer trusts the agent to act with the client's best interests in mind, to give sound advice and timely support. All of a writer's earnings pass through the agent's hands, an arrangement that can survive only where confidence is certain. The agent is the writer's representative and this means that the writer must have faith that the agent won't behave in a manner grossly inconsistent with the writer's personal ethics. The agent, meanwhile, trusts the writer to continue to produce work of the quality that brought them together in the first place, and to behave in a professional manner (abiding by contracts and not withholding or falsifying information, for example). The agent expresses, through word and deed, confidence in the writer's career, a faith that may at times have to be self-sustaining. A friendly partnership should be the immediate goal of both writer and agent—fame and fortune can tag along in time.

There are, however, built-in imbalances in almost all author-agent relationships. The writer is directly responsible for what he or she writes. Any libel suits, vicious reviews, hate mail, and ridicule that come in will be directed at the writer, not at the agent. The agent negotiates the contracts, but the author signs them and is legally bound by their clauses—the agent is not. In the end, the writer claims responsibility for the direction of his or her career, regardless of how active the agent has been as an advisor and manager; triumph and failure alike can drive even well-matched partners apart. The writer has more at stake in the partnership and is far more likely to become dependent on the relationship. Last but not least, it is the writer who pays the agent. These imbalances can remain irrelevant if both parties exercise tact and restraint—but other problems can arise.

An agent is a middleman, and must foster close ties with publishers and editors at as many houses as possible. Loyalty to the client is a first principle with every good agent, and instances of outright disloyalty are extremely rare; but when an agent is negotiating with an editor and their professional ties are close and of long standing, the edge that characterizes aggressive bargaining may sometimes be missing. No matter what the connection between agent and editor, the agent knows the perils of too often seeming intransigent, or of appearing out of touch with market realities. Writers who feel that their agents could have struck a better deal can sometimes be heard muttering about the cozy arrangements between agents and publishers—they quote fondly from Shakespeare:

> Let every eye negotiate for itself
> And trust no agent.

Or as one skeptical modern-day writer put it, "When agents and editors aren't 'doing' lunch together, they're doing deals. Agents don't like the idea of jeopardizing their free lunches—the editors *always* pay—any more than they like jeopardizing their deals."

Indeed, the agent has more than one client and will soon be back at the bargaining table representing another writer's work. When the writer and the agent first come together, the agent's attention is focused on the needs of this newest client. A few months later, when the writer discovers that the agent is often too busy with some other client to come to the phone, a certain sense of disappointment is not unusual. Signed up by a top agent from a large, powerful agency, a writer sometimes finds that he or she is eventually relegated to a younger agent relatively new to the business. If the younger agent has indeed more time and energy to devote to the writer, this may be a blessing in disguise. A first-time author who landed a prominent New York agent confessed that he was very relieved to find that most of his dealings were with the agent's assistant, herself a budding agent. "She has a few clients all her own, and though I'm not really her client, she's very helpful, always available, and not at all intimidating. But when my manuscript goes out, the cover letter is signed by *my* agent"—in other words, he can still count on a prominent agent's clout.

A good agent tries to make each client feel that he or she has the agent's undivided attention. When this illusion wears thin, as it must, the writer should remember that the agent needs to work with many clients in order to earn a living; each of those clients deserves a share of the agent's time and concern.

Agents who don't provide satisfactory service, or are unable to maintain friendly and professional relationships with their clients, quickly acquire bad reputations (as do writers who are too demanding, too temperamental). When the partnership works well, when writer and agent both do their jobs, good fellowship and good income should be the result. When either party fails, both suffer.

SPELLING OUT THE TERMS

In the past, formal contracts between author and agent were rare; the final decision to work together might have been marked by no more than a handshake and a few words about commission rates. These days more and more agents ask their clients to sign an agreement outlining the responsibilities of each party. Occasionally the contract will cover a certain time period—three years, say, with the option to renew—but it's usually open-ended, and either party may cancel with reasonable advance notice. Such a contract is no substitute for trust, good will, and professional courtesy. Nor can it be relied on as an ironclad safeguard: very rarely will either an agent or an author take the trouble (or incur the expense) of going to court to enforce a signed contract. Poets & Writers nonetheless recommends the use of some kind of written agreement, whether a formal contract or a rudimentary checklist (signed by both parties, a checklist has the same binding force as a contract).

Though the writer may argue that putting things in writing helps avoid misunderstandings, some agents won't like the idea; they may feel that the writer is betraying suspicion, that the crucial element of trust will be missing from the outset, that the author will make unreasonable demands. They may worry about the reaction of their other clients—should one author have a contract, however informal, if the others have none? A few agents may consider these points and refuse. A more common response will be relief: agents appreciate a writer with a businesslike attitude.

A checklist or other written agreement between author and agent should outline the scope of each party's responsibility to the other. Four broad topics need special attention: communication between agent and author; the types of work the agent will market; the disposition of rights; and continuing obligations should the relationship end.

Most literary agents are in New York, most writers are not; as a result, agent and author tend to communicate by letter or long-distance phone call. How often should they be in touch? What kind of news does the writer want to hear? If these questions seem too petty for serious contemplation, consider that countless writers grumble about the elusiveness of agents, and that agents, in private moments, are apt to complain about ceaseless pestering by anxious writers.

Some agents will want to handle all of a writer's work, no matter how short or how small the fee. Others will market only book-length manuscripts—the writer will have to peddle articles or short stories unassisted. Unless the writer is particularly prolific, a flexible, case-by-case arrangement usually works well.

A clear understanding of what rights, if any, the writer will *not* be assigning the agent is essential. Again, this may vary with each new manuscript, but if a general principle is stated at the outset, misunderstandings may be averted. The writer should also ask the agent about which rights he or she habitually sells to publishers, and which rights he or she likes to retain.

A contingency plan that faces squarely the possibility that the relationship may someday come to an end is actually in the best interest of both parties—neither the author nor the agent can know who, eventually, may want to leave whom.

THE NITTY-GRITTY

If the author and the agent agree to write out a checklist, here are some specific items they may want to discuss:

- The agency's commission rate for both domestic and foreign sales.
- The agent's right to a commission on work marketed by the author, for which the agent negotiates the contract; work the author markets and negotiates the contract for but which is officially represented by the agent; reprint permissions (these are usually sold not through the agent but through the publisher's permissions department).
- The author's involvement in mapping out the agent's sales pitch.
- The relative merits of exclusive submissions, multiple submissions, and auctions.
- The extent of the agent's duty as a first reader. Some encourage their clients to show them early drafts; others read only well-polished manuscripts.
- The extent of the agent's duty as watchdog over the publication process.
- The extent of the agent's duty as auxiliary publicist.
- What office expenses the agent will deduct from the writer's earnings.
- Which records the agent will keep.
- What personal information the agent may release about the author, and what information should be kept confidential.

An author's needs change as his or her career evolves; the agreement between author and agent should therefore be revised from time to time. With each new project, the author should also discuss specific marketing strategies and, once again, the disposition of specific rights.

RIGHTS FOR SALE

The total market value of a manuscript depends in part on the value of numerous subsidiary rights: film rights, TV rights, audio rights, translation rights, and so on. All these rights naturally belong to the author. But it is the agent's job, in consultation with the author, to decide what to sell when and to whom. Properly exploited, subsidiary rights can produce a handsome ancillary income. Agents earn commission on this income: 10 or 15 percent every time a subsidiary right is sold or optioned. They are therefore motivated to sell. Many good agents, in fact, thrive on the sale of subsidiary rights, especially movie and foreign rights.

Publishers are not unaware of the potential value of these rights, and when they negotiate to buy a book, they will typically try to pick up in the bargain whatever rights they can. Some rights are assigned to the hardcover publisher as a matter of course; the most important of these are trade and mass market paperback rights, and book club rights. To buy other rights, such as first serial, foreign, and audio, the publisher must offer a larger advance or some other inducement.

The publisher who snares a bundle of rights along with the manuscript is entitled to sell them to the highest bidder. The author is assigned a share of the proceeds of such sales (out of which the agent takes a commis-

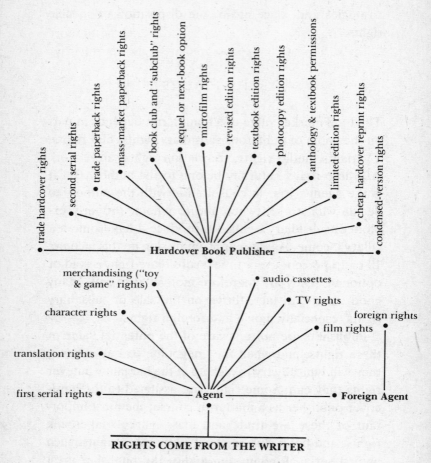

RIGHTS COME FROM THE WRITER

Rights for Sale

This diagram shows the possibilities for a successful trade book. The pattern does not hold true for every book; in fact, very few realize their potential for all twenty-two uses.

sion). When reprint rights are sold, the publisher keeps half of the money and gives half back to the author. This division of spoils also applies to the reprint royalties—the hardcover publisher takes a bite out of the author's future earnings, too. If the publisher has bought first serial rights or dramatic rights, which is unusual but not unheard of, the split is 90/10 with the author receiving the lion's share. The foreign rights split is generally 75/25.

There's a catch here. When the hardcover publisher sells off various rights, the author's share of the proceeds is paid out only *after* the original advance has been recouped. A brief example: an agent decides to give up the foreign rights to a novel when a publisher offers to buy world rights for $25,000. The publisher manages to peddle the novel in England, France, and Germany for a total of $12,000, of which $9,000 is due to the author on the basis of the 75/25 split. Not a penny will come to the author until the publisher has earned back the original $25,000 advance. If the book does well, the money will flow. But many books fail to "earn out," to use the publisher's phrase, and the rights money never materializes.

Simple arithmetic makes it plain that the writer is better served by an agent who sells foreign rights directly to the foreign publisher, first serial rights directly to the magazine or newspaper, and so on. There are times when simple arithmetic is a poor guide to action— for example, when the publisher is better equipped than the agent to sell certain rights or when the author is desperate for cash up front—but otherwise, the numbers rule.

The agent has no choice but to sell trade and mass market paperback rights to the hardcover publisher, but there's room for negotiation. Some publishers offer what are called "hard/soft deals"—they propose a larger advance in return for the right to print both hardcover and paperback editions. Agents like this kind of deal because it more or less guarantees a paperback edition and because the author receives a full royalty for every copy sold. The most common agreement, however, allows the hardcover publisher the option to sell reprint rights to another company.

These are tricky issues, complicated further by the uncertainty of any publishing effort. A good agent will explain the risks and potential benefits of selling and retaining various rights—and a responsible writer will pay close attention.

BREAKING UP IS HARD TO DO

When the author-agent relationship no longer works and the will to fix it has dissolved, it's time to get out. Too often, agent and author drift slowly apart, communication becomes strained and infrequent, both parties are unhappy, both hope for a change, but neither has the gumption to call it quits. This may sound like a certain kind of sour marriage, and indeed, the analogy extends still further: the eventual split can be messy, with enduring consequences, especially if over the years there have been many books together.

There are three common reasons for ending the relationship: the agent has been unable to sell the author's work and sees no point in making further attempts; the author is dissatisfied with the agent's efforts or attitude; or the author, having achieved a degree of success, wants a more powerful and diversified agency, a lawyer, or both.

In the first case, the agent is responsible for signing off in an honest, professional manner, and the writer for accepting the fact that not every partnership leads to success.

If the writer wishes to make a change, however, professional courtesy and practical considerations both require that the writer inform the agent of his or her decision *before* making a change. There's no point in adding insult to injury, or making an unfriendly break still more bitter; a forthright approach may smooth the negotiations that attend the dissolution of a partnership. In any event, a new agent won't represent a work until the old agent has clearly and willingly relinquished it.

Business dealings with the former agent are likely to continue. As mentioned earlier, an agent who negotiates a book contract continues to collect a commission on royalties due the author for as long as the contract remains in effect, whether or not the author is still a client. When the agent first negotiates the contract, certain rights attached to the work are relinquished to the publisher and others are retained by the agent in the author's name; unless agent and author sign an agreement that specifies otherwise, the agent has a legal right to a commission on the sale of any and all of those rights—even if the sale occurs after the agent has ceased to represent the author.

Say, for example, an agent sells a young author's first novel to a top editor at a major house. Though the agent works hard to get the best possible deal, the advance is modest; sales are, too, and the novel goes out of print. Fifteen years later, long after the author has changed agents and built a successful, lucrative career, a famous Hollywood producer offers a hefty sum for the movie rights to the author's first novel. The agent, all but forgotten, who originally marketed that manuscript is legally entitled to a commission.

The writer who quits his or her agent can ask to withdraw any unsold rights. In many cases this request is granted, but not always. In short, it's a great deal easier to fire an agent when the agent was hired with care. A final stretch of the analogy: writers who present their agents with a "pre-nuptial" agreement find that divorce is less expensive.

CHAPTER FOUR

IS THERE LIFE
BEYOND MEGABUCKS?
AGENTS AND AUTHORS
TALK ABOUT THE BUSINESS

Effective agents are usually adept at self-promotion; to counteract their enthusiasm, here's a tonic dose of skepticism from novelist and columnist Michael Thomas, who insists on the distinction between "literary agents" and "book agents": "To literary agents," he says, "the content of a book is its ideas, its narrative, its depictions, its style; to book agents the content of a book is the advance they can get for it. Literary agents by and large deal with editors; book agents deal only with the heads of houses—with whom they are always on a first-name basis. Literary agents generally read the books they represent, book agents almost never." Thomas has been represented by four different agents, including Mort Janklow and Ed Victor, two of the most powerful dealmakers in the business. He is quite certain that book agents and would-be book agents outnumber the literary kind, but this doesn't seem to bother him: "It all depends what you want out of writing. If you want readers, that's one thing; if you want dollars, that's another."

READING AGENTS, SELLING AGENTS

John Ware, himself an agent, has a more generous opinion of the profession; but he also divides his colleagues into two camps: "There are reading agents," he says, "and selling agents." The former are passionate about writing; the latter resemble Thomas's "book agents"— they revel in deal-making and disregard the quality of the prose they peddle. ("It's shocking," according to a veteran editor at a major house, "how many agents send in manuscripts they clearly haven't really read.")

The distinctions suggested by Thomas and Ware are important not because they are universally applicable— they aren't. But they do serve as a reminder that there can be a world of difference between any two agents. This is a constantly recurring refrain in any interview with an agent: *authors in search of an agent have to know what sort of partner they need and want.*

A self-described "old school" independent agent who operates as a one-man show (with a part-time assistant) out of his own apartment on the Upper West Side of New York City, John Ware doesn't at all mean to suggest that reading agents don't secure large advances for their clients—in fact, he's happy to say that he's had "a very strong year in the midst of this recession." A reading agent, he believes, can negotiate with the same determination—and the same success—as a selling agent. "You fight for the best contract," he argues, "because you love the book.

"Agenting is a life," says Ware. "A lot of agents will tell you that." In his case it seems particularly true. When he's not taking care of his fifty or sixty clients, he's sorting through the queries that come in daily over the transom. He waves in the direction of a few large but neat stacks of paper and piled-up manuscripts and explains that his authors, many of whom have become friends, don't seem to mind the "bookish mess"—"I guess they get their carpeting downtown," he adds, an oblique reference to the corporate mentality of many New York publishers. While most of his clients come through referrals, he also meets new authors at writing conferences. "A few of my major clients," he adds, "have come through the mail." Ware complains that he is besieged by phone queries. "I always say, 'Look, you and I both work with the written word. I don't charge reading fees, I usually read only on exclusive, and I need to see something in writing.' "

Ware's clients include historian Stephen E. Ambrose, social critic Alfie Kohn, and novelists Jennifer Johnston and Candida Fraze. Having worked as an editor at Doubleday for eight years and having taught a course on editing at New York University for five years, Ware considers himself an editing agent as well as a reading agent. "I have my own standard for what goes out of this office," he says. "Everything must be nailed down."

In return for his careful attention, he expects his clients to turn in manuscripts that represent their best effort. He still charges a 10-percent commission but won't rule out the possibility that someday he may start asking his new clients for 15 percent.

Many authors neither need nor desire an agent who will go over their work with a fine-tooth comb. An experienced professional writer ready to dispense with the frills is a good match for a selling agent—someone who's all action (with perhaps a hint of swagger) and who brings in the highest bid.

OVERHEAD, CLOUT, AND COST

It's a mistake to assume that only a small agency will give close attention to the text of a book. Michael Carlisle, one of the nine agents in the literary department of the William Morris Agency, argues that an author who chooses a larger agency can have the best of both worlds. At a big agency, he says, "agents are often very much on their own, almost independent. I have a tremendous amount of freedom in terms of who I decide to work with and how I choose to invest my time."

Because his agency is highly successful and financially secure (William Morris represents Tom Clancy and was responsible for concocting the *Scarlett* project, Alexandra Ripley's hugely profitable sequel to *Gone with the Wind*), Carlisle feels confident taking on unknown or obscure authors. "I think I read manuscripts differently knowing that I can take a risk. I don't have to worry about paying for the lights or the phone bill." Writers who sign on with him enlist the clout and prestige of the entire William Morris Agency.

Like most other large agencies, William Morris charges a 10-percent commission. Expenses like photocopying and postage are not deducted from the writer's earnings. All of this is in keeping with Carlisle's emphatic point: "An agent should never be somebody who's costing the writer money." Carlisle concedes, however, that financial considerations are not necessarily the most important. "In a sane publishing environment, authors would choose agents on the basis of services and compatability." The agency commission rate and ballyhooed seven-figure advances for brand-name authors would count for less than the individual agent's reputation for integrity and good judgment. "The writer should scrutinize the agent very carefully," says Carlisle, who represents some eighty clients, including John Casey and Leon Edel. "What is the writer looking for? Some people want an agent who is a reflection of their own persona as they perceive it. Others want somebody who is meaner and tougher than themselves. If you're serious about your work, you'd better be serious about who speaks up for you."

Most small and midsize independent agents charge a 15-percent commission. To run even a modest office, especially in Manhattan, is an expensive proposition. Jean Naggar points out that "an agent who has to take on more and more writers just to keep up with overhead isn't working well for anyone. An agent who charges 15 percent presumably can give more attention to fewer writers."

Elaine Markson, who founded her own agency in 1972, makes a similar argument when she points out that "there are plenty of agents who can sell for you. What it really boils down to is the relationship the writer has with the agent." She cites approvingly the caution of a new client, short-story writer David Wong Louie: "He interviewed seven different agents, and came back to see me three times before making up his mind. He was looking for a personal relationship that was right for him."

Markson has seven employees, two of whom are full-time agents, and her agency represents about 180 clients, among them Alice Hoffman and Frederick Busch; that's a fairly typical size for a well-established independent New York agency. In the comfortable disarray of her Greenwich Village offices she talks about the importance an agent can assume during the course of a writer's career. "Agents remain in place," she says. "Editors are constantly moving, publishers close down or get bought—people get fired—so the person you turn to, the constant, is your agent."

Like many agents, Markson can't help steering the conversation in the direction of her own authors and their various projects. She tells the story of a book that was first placed at a major publishing house with an editor who left, then taken over by another editor, who was fired, and next handled by a third editor, who came and went in a matter of weeks. "So far there have been four editors," she exclaims, "and the author hasn't even delivered the manuscript yet. And this is a big, big book for which they paid a lot of money." As the round robin of editors goes on, the agent is always there, to make sure the publishing process goes smoothly.

FURS AND FRIENDSHIP

Novelist Mona Simpson didn't do much in the way of choosing her agent, Amanda "Binky" Urban of International Creative Management, but the partnership— now a friendship—has lasted for ten stable years. "I signed with Binky very early on in my career," says Simpson. "I wasn't looking for an agent or even thinking of one." An editor at *The Atlantic Monthly* sent a few of Simpson's stories to Urban. "She liked them," Simpson explains, "and so she called me out of the blue when I was still in graduate school. Oh boy, I thought, *an agent called.* She took me to lunch somewhere very fancy. She was very glamorous—she had this fur coat, and I was in sneakers. So you see I never really thought about it—I met Binky and she said she wanted to represent me and I said great.

"I would have wanted an agent eventually anyway. There are a lot of writers who are genuinely interested in the business side of things and read *Publishers Weekly* regularly. But I'm not inclined that way—I'd just as soon let Binky take care of all that." Simpson's good fortune in falling into a successful relationship is less common than her attitude toward the nitty-gritty of publishing—contract clauses and royalty scales.

Elaine Markson argues that the agent acts as an essential buffer between the representatives of the publishing company and the writer. This role is important when the contract is negotiated, says Markson, because "most editors hate talking about money with writers, and most writers aren't very good at it." When the writer delivers the book to the editor, the situation arises again: "If there's some problem with the manuscript, if the editor is unhappy for some reason, the agent gets a call." The agent mediates in the discussions that follow, taking the writer's side in case of disagreement—unless the editor has contributed a valid and important point. When at last the publisher sends along the royalty statements, the agent dons a new hat: translator. Commenting on the painful obscurity of these documents, Markson says flatly, "No other business would dare send out statements like these."

But of all her duties, reading takes up the most time. "The good agents," she declares, "never stop reading."

Her colleagues Virginia Barber and Jean Naggar would certainly agree. Though Naggar and Barber both run agencies slightly smaller than Markson's, Naggar reports that her office receives roughly five thousand queries per year; Barber struggles with nearly the same load—about eighty-five per week. And then there are the manuscripts their own authors produce, sometimes a total of more than twenty per year. Both try hard to limit the number of writers on their list (Barber's agency handles some 70 clients, Naggar's 110), but opportunities arise—an accomplished writer goes shopping for a new agent, for instance—that seem impossible to refuse. Moreover, even busy, prominent agents such as these do on occasion find an author in the "slush pile"— the stack of unsolicited queries—and agree to make room for the new arrival.

When Virginia Barber, whose more established clients include Anne Rivers Siddons, Alice Munro, and Nicholas von Hoffman, talks about an unknown prospect, her excitement sweeps her along: "We've got somebody right now who is complete slush, and we're trying to find him and say we want to represent him. He sent in a one-paragraph letter—the odds against this are so long I'm absolutely staggered. It was a description of his novel; it was so laconic, so to the point." Her assistant asked to see the complete manuscript, read it, and then passed it to Barber without comment— "She just said, 'I want you to read this.' I loved it," says Barber, and explains that the author is somewhere in Europe. "We don't know him, he doesn't know us. I don't know how old he is, where he came from, whether he's American, whether it's all a hoax. I have a lot of investigating to do—because the book is that good. If it works out, it will be the story of the year for us."

Each of the four first novels Jean Naggar represented in 1990–91 came to her through an unsolicited query; not one of the queries was seconded by a recommendation. Naggar stresses this last point because "people in other cities are somewhat obsessed with the idea that if you don't live in New York and you don't have lots of contacts, you won't get a fair reading." If the query is compelling, the agent won't care about the zip code on the return address.

"One thing agents can do for a beginning writer," says author Harold Brodkey, "is to give an imprimatur. The agent says this person is okay, and that gives the editors courage." He adds that his own agent, Andrew Wylie, is "the intelligent, commonsensical, legally and commercially well-informed side of me that I really ought to have as part of my self but I just don't."

SHARING SUCCESS

Authors are not the only ones to benefit from a successful partnership: launching a writer can transform an agent's career as well. Jean Naggar's reputation received a tremendous boost in 1979 when she sold Jean Auel's *Clan of the Cave Bear* to Crown for $130,000— at the time a record price for a first novel by an unknown writer. Auel's most recent contract, negotiated by Naggar in the last months of 1989, was one of the richest in the history of publishing. The fact that Naggar "discovered" Auel, and has continued to pick winners over the years, has led many publishers to respect her judgment.

Sandra Dijkstra, who started her agency in 1983 in Del Mar, California, also had a leg-up from a first-time novelist. "I had to invent the wheel out here," she says of her early years as a West Coast agent. "There was no reason why I should have been successful—I wasn't in New York, I came from an academic background, and I had no publishing experience." A San Diego radio show about books earned her some visibility, but it was a slow beginning. "Any agent who's just starting out is selecting dreck from the dreck," she notes.

In 1987 Dijkstra agreed to represent a young writer named Amy Tan with one published story to her credit and two others, unpublished, in hand. In October of that year, after Tan had written a proposal for a book-length series of interconnected stories, Dijkstra set to work. A Knopf editor offered $15,000; Dijkstra refused—a gamble, considering that her client had only thirty pages on paper. Knopf raised the ante to $20,000 but asked for both hard- and softcover rights. The safe tactic at this point would have been to accept gratefully, but Dijkstra again refused; she was after an offer that would allow her client to write full-time. In the end Putnam bid $50,000 for North American hardcover rights; Doubleday suggested a two-book deal, $135,000 for world hardcover rights. "It was a terribly difficult decision," Dijkstra recalls, "and Amy said, 'You decide.' I told her, 'Trust me—we'll take the one-book offer and we'll do better next time around.' " She adds, "Many people in New York thought I was being unreasonable asking for so much money. Some thought I was insane."

When *The Joy Luck Club* rocketed up the best-seller list, and the paperback rights were sold at auction for more than $1.2 million, Dijkstra knew that her several gambles had paid off—and so did the rest of the publishing community. Dijkstra now represents about one

hundred authors, including Susan Faludi and novelist
Robert Ferrigno. As for Tan, she told a *New York
Times* reporter that she gave thanks to her agent "for
saving my life."

These are exceptional deals, the kind most agents
and all but a few writers merely dream about. However,
as "literary" or "reading" agents are quick to point out,
it's not a good idea to dream only of dollar amounts.
"Quite frankly," says Virginia Barber, "there are occasions when what you need to do is get the most money
possible for the author. But there are other occasions
when the author badly needs a good, supportive editor.
It's terrible for an agent to treat every project alike"—
and that, according to many agents, can be the sad result
of the frenzied pursuit of big-money advances.

BEYOND MEGABUCKS

Perry Knowlton has been an agent at Curtis Brown,
Ltd., a large New York agency, since 1959. Before that
he was an editor at Charles Scribner's Sons. With a
total of thirty-nine years in the business, he can lay claim
to a historical perspective. "The huge advances," he
declares, "have done more than anything to hurt the
publishing industry and drive it into what is really a
major recession." In the early 1960s Knowlton sold the
novel *Fail Safe,* by Eugene Burdick and Harvey
Wheeler, for $50,000—at that point the largest advance
ever negotiated by a Curtis Brown agent. Today it's a
paltry sum. Knowlton points to the deal struck in the

summer of 1990 between HarperCollins and popular
British writer Jeffrey Archer: $20 million for two novels
and a collection of stories. "This kind of megabucks
deal is just terrible," says Knowlton. "The books will
never earn out, and it's taken a huge amount of working
capital away from HarperCollins—money that could be
used to buy many, many good books. It hurts the industry all the way down."

For Knowlton, who represents some thirty active authors, including Robertson Davies, Judith McNaught,
and Alvin Toffler, the agent's job, properly construed,
involves building careers. He likes to say that "at Curtis
Brown we sign up authors, we don't sign up books."
As an example, he cites the case of his client Tony
Hillerman, whose mysteries sold well, but not spectac-
ularly, as genre novels in the mid-1980s. Knowlton,
along with Hillerman's hardcover editor, Lawrence P.
Ashmead of HarperCollins, spent a good deal of time
discussing ways to swell Hillerman's audience. At last
they hit upon the idea of reprinting the novels not in a
mass market edition but in the more expensive trade
paperback format. Not only did Hillerman catch on with
the upmarket trade paperback buyers, but those same
buyers pushed subsequent hardcovers onto the best-
seller list. "Now Tony always makes the list," says
Knowlton, "all his novels are back in print, and every-
body's happy."

If an agent is to help build the writer's career, the
relationship must be made of sturdy, lasting stuff.
Knowlton has no prescription for how to make the bond
endure. "What makes a marriage work?" he asks. "I

have no idea, but the same things that tear up a marriage can tear up the relationship between an author and his agent." Like John Ware, he believes that good agents are dedicated to agenting, that it becomes their life.

Most agents encourage early and far-reaching discussions of the relationship's parameters. Whether or not they are used to signing contracts or written agreements with their clients, they want the author to know what an agent's services entail, how commissions work, how subsidiary rights are best exploited.

John Ware has never signed a contract with a client— "I'd be willing, but nobody has ever asked," he says. Nor does he feel that written agreements are particularly important, because the legal essentials of an author-agent relationship are codified in the agent clause of every publisher's contract. "The rest," he argues, "is largely procedural." He nonetheless expects to reach a clear understanding of both parties' duties and responsibilities with every client he accepts.

THE AGENT'S MANTRA: PASSION FOR THE WORK

Ware's description of what he expects from the author is direct and to the point: "I want the writer to give me his best shot." This sentiment is echoed by other agents who argue that the author must start out by showing respect for his or her own work—it's otherwise difficult for the agent to express the enthusiasm necessary to market the manuscript. "I sell on my passion for the work" is a phrase repeated like a mantra at agencies all over the country.

The corollary to that well-worn proposition is that when the passion flags, or dries up entirely, the agent can't perform. Elaine Markson had a client whose first novel she had sold happily and successfully. He recently brought in his second effort, which Markson read and promptly refused to represent. "He was terribly disappointed, but I said, 'How can I sell something I hate?' It was an awfully violent book—though I'm sure he'll find another agent very easily." Less extreme cases can also damage the relationship. When the agent doesn't show enthusiasm, or when the writer suspects that the enthusiasm simply isn't there, problems are likely to emerge. Markson remembers an accomplished writer who came to her looking to change agents. She asked what the trouble was with his current arrangement and discovered that the writer felt that he wasn't properly appreciated. "I made him go back to his agent. I said, 'I know your agent, and I know how she loves your work. You may be hitting a bad patch just now in terms of publishing, but you have an agent who is out there beating the drums for you.' "

Misunderstandings are inevitable without good communication. Virginia Barber stresses the importance of "an open, direct, and candid relationship." Says Jean Naggar, "If you have a problem with an agent, take the time and trouble to communicate it to the agent—who is probably overworked, and so on. If you find it difficult to get in touch with your agent," she adds, "then you do have a problem." Michael Carlisle offers this gloomy but nonetheless useful advice: "If you have an instinct that something's wrong, it probably is."

Even when the relationship works smoothly, bad luck, bad timing, and the bitter realities of the marketplace can break it up. Barber offers the example of her failed attempt to sell a book by Charles Baxter. "I was his first agent, and I cannot tell you how much I loved his short stories. But he had a novel to sell, and I just couldn't sell it—in fact it never was sold. Anyway—I gave up, and later he went on to another agent and sold a collection of stories. And I think he's fabulous."

Baxter acknowledges that Barber "did her very best by me." He remembers that he'd been writing for a while when he was recommended to Barber: "I was in my early thirties, but I don't think my work was publishable. She saw some good things in it, but she couldn't sell it, and I came to realize that I needed to start all over again, to relearn the craft." Five years later he signed with a new agent, Liz Darhansoff, who sold his story collection to Viking. Looking back on the early years of his career, Baxter remarks, "At a time when I really ought to have been writing and learning how to do it, I was like everyone else—I wanted to sell it. But I didn't know—because no writer really knows these things—that I wasn't ready. It's painful to discover that people don't want to buy your writing, but it usually does mean something."

Authors are not alone in suffering from rejection. Sandra Dijkstra remembers that her first major client dropped her after just one book. More bad timing—

the author, having reached the cusp of fame, moved on to sign up with a famous agent at a venerable agency.

But for every sad story about an opportunity missed, a talent spurned, or a friendly partnership dissolved, agents tell ten more about the rewards of perseverance, the satisfaction of seeing excellence recognized, and the solid pleasure of doing business so that all sides win. It's hard to find an agent who doesn't have a ready anecdote about the writer whose manuscript traveled endlessly—*"Thirty-four publishers rejected it!"*—before eventually finding its home and, once published, winning a bouquet of distinguished prizes.

CHAPTER FIVE

OTHER AVENUES: LAWYERS AND LECTURE BUREAUS

THE LAWYER-AGENT

Any writer confident of securing a very substantial advance for his or her manuscript may want to consider a compromise between hiring an agent on a commission basis and doing entirely without. There are a few dozen lawyers, most of them in major cities, who regularly represent authors in contract negotiations with publishers. These lawyer-agents offer some of the same services as an agent, but instead of charging a commission, they bill their clients on a per-hour basis. This arrangement works especially well for celebrity authors—individuals whose name alone is likely to excite the interest of a publisher.

Lawyer-agents will offer to market a manuscript

(though the net they cast may not be as wide as that of a good literary agent); to haggle with the editor over contractual clauses; and to settle any disputes that may arise during the publishing process. Some are even ready to provide editorial counsel. The bill for their services reflects the time they spend on the job, not the kind of work they do, or the success they meet with. An agent who works on a commission basis, on the other hand, only earns money when the writer does.

Though they may be expert negotiators, most lawyer-agents don't have a literary agent's familiarity with the ins and outs of the publishing community. If a writer needs to be matched with an editor, and the match-making is likely to be a complicated affair, it's better to hire an expert. Lawyer-agents also tend to sell the publisher rights that a literary agent would retain, which in some cases will prove a distinct disadvantage. An effective literary agent can sell rights worldwide and produce considerable revenue. Publishers often aren't as successful at selling subsidiary rights as a committed agent. In addition, they generally withhold the proceeds from sub-rights sales until the book has earned back its advance, and they take a larger cut of that income than a literary agent does.

The writer who is represented by a lawyer will have to monitor royalty statements, keep records, and handle business correspondence, tasks that would otherwise fall to the agent. Also, a good literary agent is probably better equipped than even the best lawyer-agent to give a client long-term advice about managing a career.

To all of these objections, lawyer-agents have a sim-

ple answer: they save their clients money. The bigger
the deal, the bigger the savings. One Washington-based
lawyer-agent who mostly represents the work of political figures and broadcast journalists charges $375 an
hour. He argues that his fee is in effect quite modest.
Most literary agents would collect $300,000 on a
$2 million contract; when he negotiated a deal of that
size, he was paid slightly less than $30,000. One of his
clients, a television news personality, earned a total of
about $275,000 from a best-selling memoir. The stan-
dard 15-percent commission on income of $275,000
would be $41,250; the lawyer-agent's bill came to
$11,000. "You've got to look at the bottom line," says
the happy newscaster. "He's a superbargain."

However, if the author's advance comes to less than
$75,000, a $375-per-hour fee begins to seem relatively
expensive. Marketing a book and negotiating a contract
take a certain amount of time regardless of the money
involved.

THE LECTURE AGENT

With the proliferation of writing workshops, conferences, and seminars, new opportunities arise for the
established writer: invitations to read, lecture, and
teach. Some of these, especially the short-term teaching
assignments, pay fairly well, and public appearances can
help sell a writer's books. There are two ways to take
advantage of these opportunities: make use of the relevant published material (the Poets & Writers book

Author & Audience: A Readings and Workshop Guide,
for example, lists the sponsors of more than six hundred
reading series) or hire a lecture agent.

Lecture agents are most useful for celebrities and
nonfiction writers with up-to-the-minute and controversial topics. Poets and fiction writers, unless they are
in great demand, are probably better off sticking to the
do-it-yourself method, though that approach takes
time, careful organization, and a talent for self-
promotion.

The immediate disadvantage of lecture agents is that
they charge hefty commissions: anywhere from 25 to
40 percent of the client's fee. To compensate for the
lost income, the writer may have to inflate his or her
fee or accept many more engagements. The first solu-
tion may price the writer out of the market (why hire
one author for the price of two?); and the second may
involve a taxing schedule (when will the author find
time to write?). On the other hand, a good lecture agent
may be able to arrange just the right number of well-
paid appearances—more than enough to cover the
added cost of the commission. And a lecture agent, like
a literary agent, is responsible for handling the many
business details an author may prefer to ignore.

The 1992 *Literary Market Place* listed nine lecture
agents, but that list is far from complete. In major cities,
the yellow pages of the telephone book should provide
the names of a few agencies under "Lecture Bureaus"
or "Agents (Lecture)." Like literary agents, lecture
agents will only represent an author if they think the
commissions will be worthwhile. Some insist on exclu-

sivity—that is, they ask that all the writer's paid appearances be booked through the agency. Most require a written contract specifying a one- to three-year commitment.

Here are some points the contract should cover:

- the rate of commission
- the payment schedule (some lecture agents are slow to pass on their clients' earnings)
- what costs, if any, will be billed to the client (promotion, office expenses)
- the terms of exclusivity (what kinds of speaking engagements must be booked through the agent)
- duration of the contract

Writers should scrutinize lecture agents as they would literary agents. References from clients are useful, but the most reliable source of information may be sponsors or administrators who organize lecture series. If the lecture agent has a good reputation, then the only question remaining is whether the writer and the agent are likely to get along; a few telephone conversations or, if practical, a face-to-face meeting should provide the answer.

CHAPTER SIX

THE FEE-CHARGING AGENT: DOES ANY WRITER NEED ONE?

Thirty-seven of the 233 agents surveyed in this book charge a reading fee; they are listed beginning on page 161. A fee-charging agent will ask for money up front in return for handling, reading, and criticizing a writer's manuscript. If and when the agent deems the manuscript ready for submission, he or she is supposed to market it to publishers. But though they call themselves agents, many of the people who offer these services are more like free-lance editors. Their principal source of income, by and large, is not the commission on works they have sold but the reading fees collected from would-be authors.

LET THE BUYER BEWARE!

The reader's fee can work like a cat's paw, prying money from writers who can scarce afford shoddy services of dubious value. It's an easy scam for quasi-literary charlatans. One fee-charging agent is known to have paid mailroom employees at various publishing houses for the names and addresses on rejected manuscripts—bruised by rejection, these disappointed writers must have seemed easy targets for mail solicitation.

Fee-charging agencies also advertise their services, a tactic unknown among reputable agents, who rely on word of mouth and professional listings to attract new clients. (A fee-charging agency that advertises and neglects to say in the advertisement that a fee may be required is breaking the law.)

A few larger agencies do two kinds of business: the literary department is composed of commission agents, and a wholly separate department is staffed with readers hired to evaluate, for a fee, the load of unsolicited manuscripts. Typically, the fee-charging department thrives thanks to the reputation of the commission agents, whose successes are trumpeted in the agency's advertisements. But the commission agents seldom see, let alone market, any of the profit-making slush sent in by writers duped by these ads.

The Association of Authors' Representatives (AAR), formed in 1991 after the merger of the sixty-three-year-old Society of Author's Representatives (SAR) and the fourteen-year-old Independent Literary Agents Association (ILAA), takes a dim view of reading fees. The old SAR did not admit fee-charging members. ILAA allowed the practice (some 10 to 15 percent of its members charged reading fees) but formulated a set of strict guidelines. Here, slightly abridged, are the relevant passages from the ILAA code of ethics.

> ILAA believes that the practice of literary agents charging clients or potential clients fees for reading and evaluating literary works . . . is subject to serious abuse. . . . For this reason, ILAA discourages that practice. ILAA members who do charge such fees are required to comply with the following:
> 1. Before entering into any agreement whereby a fee is to be charged for reading and evaluating any work, the member must provide to the author a written statement that clearly sets forth (a) the nature and extent of the services to be rendered . . . (b) whether the services are to be rendered by the member personally, and if not, a description of the professional background of the person who will render the services; (c) the period of time within which the services will be rendered; (d) under what circumstances, if any, the fee will be refunded to the author; (e) the amount of the fee, including any initial payment as well as any other payments that may be requested by the member for additional services . . . and (f) that the rendering of such services shall not guarantee that the member will agree to represent the author or will render the work more salable to publishers.

Further provisions require fee-charging ILAA agents to indicate in any published professional listing that they charge a fee. They are also prohibited from advertising or otherwise soliciting reading-fee submissions. A final clause insists that reading for a fee "shall not constitute more than an incidental part of the member's professional activity."

The AAR has admitted to its ranks the few ILAA-affiliated agents who do charge fees. The association will not, however, allow new fee-charging agents to join. AAR policy on this matter is subject to review in 1993.

There are some honorable and effective fee-charging agents. Younger agents sometimes charge fees when they are just starting out and then abandon the practice when they begin to earn substantial commissions. A writer who sends out a number of queries may stumble on an agent who asks for a fee. The writer, in return, can withdraw the manuscript, even if it's been "accepted," or buy the services offered. Before giving money to a fee-charging agent, the writer should be satisfied that the agent is living up to the spirit, at least, of the ILAA provisions. A written statement describing fees and services is essential.

Reading fees can be nominal or they can be very expensive. They typically range from $25 to cover the cost of handling a submission to $500 or more for a long manuscript. An agency that accepts a fee in advance and then fails to deliver a promised evaluation is breaking the law. Withholding any prepaid service for longer than three months is illegal unless the customer is allowed to cancel the order and get a refund.

Writers who hire fee-charging agents probably hope to see their manuscript published; all they're likely to get is an editorial evaluation. If the agent does send out the manuscript, in most cases it won't get a warm reception: editors are used to halfhearted submissions of poor-quality material from agents who market rights only as a sideline. Unscrupulous fee-charging agents have been known to pass manuscripts on to vanity publishers, who offer to print the author's work—to the tune of several thousand dollars.

WHAT IF A WRITER *NEEDS* EDITORIAL HELP?

Agents and editors have very different jobs. While many agents say that more and more they are assuming an editorial role (they claim to shape their clients' proposals and polish their manuscripts), the essential distinction has not changed: an agent represents an author's work; an editor edits it for publication. If an agent markets a manuscript, a commission should be the reward for success. If an agent reads and evaluates a manuscript, the professional titles have been misappropriated—the agent is in fact an editor.

A writer who needs help with a manuscript can always hire an accredited professional. There are 441 free-lance editors listed in the 1992 *Literary Market Place*; all of them have references from publishers—a condition for making the list. A cross-index establishes specialties: 212 entries under manuscript analysis, 229 under line editing. These editors can be as expensive as fee-charging agents, or more so. Some of them may not be particularly good at their job. But there is no confusion as to their identity or the category of service they provide.

Writing workshops, seminars, and conferences— nearly four hundred per year according to the 1992 *Guide to Writers' Conferences* published by the Shaw Association—are offered all over the country and in all seasons. The May issues of *Writer's Digest* and *The Writer* list most of the writers' conferences held in the United States and abroad. Poets & Writers also publishes an annual annotated list each March. Many of the conferences attract publishers, editors, and literary agents, all of whom are there in part to scout out new talent. The help available to a writer at workshops and conferences may not be as precise or as practically useful as the recommendations of a free-lance editor, but the experience can be both enjoyable and fruitful.

LITERARY AGENCIES:
AN ANNOTATED LIST

The 196 literary agencies listed here will consider un-solicited—that is, unreferred—material without charging a reading fee. In almost all cases these agents want to see queries and proposals first, *not* complete manuscripts, and they much prefer mail queries over telephone queries.

Always, always enclose a self-addressed, stamped envelope when writing to an agent. Material sent without an SASE will most often be discarded without a reply.

Writers may want to note that most agents consider a "reading" and an "evaluation" as two quite separate tasks. A manuscript turned down by an agent will most likely come back with nothing more than a polite "no thanks." This is partly because an agent does not have time to comment on rejected manuscripts, but also because personal taste and market realities play a large part in an agent's decision. As one agent said, "If I don't want to represent a manuscript, it doesn't mean it's not good." Some agencies, however, will provide a written evaluation of a rejected manuscript, for a fee. When questioned, these agents said they had developed such a strategy in response to writers who requested manuscript evaluations. "It's not a business we prefer to do," said one agent, "so we are willing to offer the service but not to finance it." Since these agencies do *read* manuscripts without charge, they are included here.

Many agencies do not charge for any services. At others, clients may be required to reimburse the agency for expenses such as long-distance telephone calls, photocopying, and postage. Usually these reimbursements are paid only after the agent makes a sale, but in some cases agencies require of new clients an up-front "contract fee" or a fee against future commissions or to cover marketing costs (again, telephone, postage, and photocopying are cited). Writers offered representation in such a case will have to weigh the value of the agent's efforts against such a fee. Again, since those agencies do read manuscripts without charge, we have included them here.

This list was compiled from questionnaires Poets & Writers, Inc., sent to all 472 literary agencies listed in the 1991 *Literary Market Place* (R.R. Bowker Company, 1991). 240 agencies—51 percent—responded.

Acton & Dystel ————
928 Broadway
Suite 303
New York, NY 10010
Phone: (212) 473-1700 Fax: (212) 505-0278

Contact: Jane Dystel, Jay Acton
Agency Commission: 15%
Manuscript categories represented:
Fiction, nonfiction.
Agency accepts:
  Telephone Queries: Y   Unsolicited Mss: Y
      Mail Queries: Y   Poetry Collections: N

Lee Allan Agency
P.O. Box 18617
Milwaukee, WI 53218
Phone: (414) 357-7708

Contact: Lee Matthias
Agency Commission: 10%–20%
Manuscript categories represented:
Book-length fiction, nonfiction, and feature-length screenplays. Specializes in genre fiction and commercial screenplays. No plays, poetry, or anthologies.
Agency accepts:
  Telephone Queries: N   Unsolicited Mss: N
      Mail Queries: Y   Poetry Collections: N

James Allen Literary Agency
538 East Hartford Street
Milford, PA 18337
Phone: (717) 296-6205 Fax: (717) 296-7266

Contact: James Allen
Agency Commission: 10% U.S., 20% abroad, film
Manuscript categories represented:
  All, except Westerns, pornography, contemporary category romance. Specializes in science fiction, fantasy, mainstream.
Agency accepts:
  Telephone Queries: N   Unsolicited Mss: N
        Mail Queries: Y   Poetry Collections: N

Marcia Amsterdam Agency
41 West 82nd Street
New York, NY 10024
Phone: (212) 873-4945 Fax: (212) 873-4945

Contact: Marcia Amsterdam
Agency Commission: 15% U.S., 10% films and TV, 20% abroad
Manuscript categories represented:
  All.
Agency accepts:
  Telephone Queries: N   Unsolicited Mss: N
        Mail Queries: Y   Poetry Collections: N

Bart Andrews & Associates, Inc.
1321 North Stanley Avenue
Los Angeles, CA 90046
Phone: (213) 851-8158 Fax: (213) 851-9738

Contact: Bart Andrews
Agency Commission: 15%

Manuscript categories represented:
Biography, how-to, humor, true crime, film and television history. Specializes in show business books, especially unauthorized biographies and celebrity autobiographies.
Agency accepts:

| Telephone Queries: N | Unsolicited Mss: N |
| Mail Queries: Y | Poetry Collections: N |

The Axelrod Agency
66 Church Street
Lenox, MA 01240
Phone: (413) 637-2000 Fax: (413) 637-4725

Contact: Steven Axelrod
Agency Commission: 10% U.S., 20% abroad
Manuscript categories represented:
All but science fiction and Westerns. Specializes in women's fiction and general nonfiction.
Agency accepts:

| Telephone Queries: Y | Unsolicited Mss: Y |
| Mail Queries: Y | Poetry Collections: N |

Julian Bach Literary Agency, Inc.
22 East 71 Street
New York, NY 10021
Phone: (212) 772-8900 Fax: (212) 772-2617

Contact: Julian Bach, Emma Sweeney
Agency Commission: 15%
Manuscript categories represented:

Fiction, nonfiction. Does not accept poetry, short stories, photography books, science fiction, children's books, inspirational, religious, horror.

Agency accepts:

Telephone Queries: N	Unsolicited Mss: N
Mail Queries: Y	Poetry Collections: N

Malaga Baldi Literary Agency, Inc.

Box 591, Radio City Station
New York, NY 10101
Phone: (212) 222-1221

Contact: Malaga Baldi
Agency Commission: 15%
Manuscript categories represented:

Literary fiction and nonfiction. Does not accept young adult, science fiction, adventure, fantasy, children's books, romance. "Prefer to read full fiction manuscript. Send SAS postcard if you want to know that the manuscript has been received. Allow 10 weeks minimum. Prefer mail queries."

Agency accepts:

Telephone Queries: Y	Unsolicited Mss: Y
Mail Queries: Y	Poetry Collections: N

The Balkin Agency, Inc.

317 South Pleasant Street
Amherst, MA 01002
Phone: (413) 256-1934 Fax: (413) 256-1935

Contact: Richard Balkin
Agency Commission: 15% U.S., 20% abroad

Manuscript categories represented:
Adult nonfiction, reference, college text. "My favorites are American history, popular culture, science, natural history, biography, film."
Agency accepts:

Telephone Queries: N	Unsolicited Mss: N
Mail Queries: Y	Poetry Collections: N

Virginia Barber Literary Agency, Inc.

101 Fifth Avenue, Suite 11-F
New York, NY 10003
Phone: (212) 255-6515 Fax: (212) 691-9418

Contact: Virginia Barber, Mary Evans, Jennifer R. Walsh
Agency Commission: 15%
Manuscript categories represented:
"Looking for upscale literary fiction and nonfiction."
Agency accepts:

Telephone Queries: N	Unsolicited Mss: N
Mail Queries: Y	Poetry Collections: N

Helen Barrett Literary Agency

175 West 13th Street
New York, NY 10011
Phone: (212) 645-7430

Contact: Helen Barrett
Agency Commission: 15% U.S., 20% abroad
Manuscript categories represented:
Mainstream fiction and nonfiction. Takes phone queries only from published writers.

Agency accepts:
Telephone Queries: N   Unsolicited Mss: N
      Mail Queries: Y   Poetry Collections: N

Loretta Barrett Books, Inc.
121 West 27th Street
Suite 601
New York, NY 10001
Phone: (212) 242-3420 Fax: (212) 727-0280

Contact: Morgan Barnes
Agency Commission: 15% U.S., 20% abroad
Manuscript categories represented:
   General trade—in particular, serious nonfiction and
   women's fiction.
Agency accepts:
Telephone Queries: N   Unsolicited Mss: N
      Mail Queries: Y   Poetry Collections: N

Maximilian Becker
115 East 82nd Street
New York, NY 10028
Phone: (212) 988-3887

Contact: Maximilian Becker, Aleta Daley
Agency Commission: 15% U.S., 20% abroad
Manuscript categories represented:
   "Our interests are eclectic. Although we are primarily
   interested in trade books, we represent scholarly
   works as well."
Agency accepts:

Telephone Queries: Y   Unsolicited Mss: N
Mail Queries: Y   Poetry Collections: Y

Does not charge a reading fee. However, if the writer wants a critique or thorough analysis, a fee is charged. The fee varies according to length of manuscript, the extent of problems or weaknesses, whether the writer wants a page-by-page analysis or a 3- to 4-page critique of the whole.

Vicky Bijur Literary Agency

333 West End Avenue
New York, NY 10023
Phone: (212) 580-4108 Fax: (212) 496-1572

Contact: Vicky Bijur
Agency Commission: 15% U.S., 20% abroad
Manuscript categories represented:
   All types of nonfiction. Almost all fiction handled is mystery genre. The only children's titles handled are nonfiction.
Agency accepts:
   Telephone Queries: Y   Unsolicited Mss: N
   Mail Queries: Y   Poetry Collections: N

The Blake Group Literary Agency

One Turtle Creek Village
Suite 600
Dallas, TX 75219
Phone: (214) 520-8562

Contact: (Mrs.) Lee B. Halff
Agency Commission: 10%, all sales

Manuscript categories represented:
General fiction. Nonfiction: how-to, self-help, cookbooks. Children's literature and juvenile.
Agency accepts:
Telephone Queries: Y   Unsolicited Mss: N
Mail Queries: Y   Poetry Collections: Y

Reid Boates Literary Agency
Box 328
274 Cooks Crossroad
Pittstown, NJ 08867-0328
Phone: (908) 730-8523 Fax: (908) 730-8931

Contact: Reid Boates
Agency Commission: 15% U.S., 20% abroad
Manuscript categories represented:
General fiction and nonfiction. Specialize in biography, autobiography, memoirs, current affairs, investigative true crime, business, and major books on health and wellness.
Agency accepts:
Telephone Queries: N   Unsolicited Mss: N
Mail Queries: Y   Poetry Collections: N

Bookmark: The Literary Agency
P.O. Box 170
Irvington-on-Hudson, NY 10533
Phone: (914) 345-9125 Fax: (914) 345-9154

Contact: Donald Cutler
Agency Commission: 10% U.S., 20% abroad
Manuscript categories represented:

All types except juvenile books.

Agency accepts:

Telephone Queries: Y	Unsolicited Mss: Y
Mail Queries: Y	Poetry Collections: N

Georges Borchardt, Inc.

136 East 57th Street
New York, NY 10022
Phone: (212) 753-5785 Fax: (212) 838-6518

Contact: Georges Borchardt
Agency Commission: 10% U.S., 15% British, 20% translation
Manuscript categories represented:
Fiction and nonfiction.

Agency accepts:

Telephone Queries: N	Unsolicited Mss: N
Mail Queries: N	Poetry Collections: N

Brandt & Brandt Literary Agents, Inc.

1501 Broadway
New York, NY 10036
Phone: (212) 840-5760 Fax: (212) 840-5776

Contact: Carl Brandt
Agency Commission: 10%
Manuscript categories represented:
Fiction and nonfiction.

Agency accepts:

Telephone Queries: N	Unsolicited Mss: N
Mail Queries: Y	Poetry Collections: N

The Joan Brandt Agency
697 West End Avenue
New York, NY 10025
Phone: (212) 749-4771 Fax: (212) 678-4588

Contact: Joan Brandt
Agency Commission: 15%
Manuscript categories represented:
  Fiction, popular nonfiction.
Agency accepts:
  Telephone Queries: N   Unsolicited Mss: N
          Mail Queries: Y   Poetry Collections: N

Andrea Brown Literary Agency, Inc.
1081 Alameda
Suite 71
Belmont, CA 94002
Phone: (415) 508-8410 Fax: (415) 592-8846

Contact: Andrea Brown
Agency Commission: 15%
Manuscript categories represented:
  Juvenile. Interested only in material for middle
  grades and nonfiction.
Agency accepts:
  Telephone Queries: Y   Unsolicited Mss: N
          Mail Queries: N   Poetry Collections: N

Curtis Brown, Ltd.
10 Astor Place
New York, NY 10003
Phone: (212) 473-5400

Contact: Laura Blake
Agency Commission: not specified
Manuscript categories represented:
General trade fiction and nonfiction, juvenile. "Always query first."
Agency accepts:

Telephone Queries: N   Unsolicited Mss: N
Mail Queries: Y   Poetry Collections: N

Marie Brown Associates
625 Broadway
Room 902
New York, NY 10012
Phone: (212) 533-5534 Fax: (212) 533-0849

Contact: Marie Brown
Agency Commission: 15%
Manuscript categories represented:
Fiction, nonfiction, and children's books. Specializes in African-American culture, women's interests, books for young readers, multicultural interests. Representation of poetry is very limited.
Agency accepts:

Telephone Queries: N   Unsolicited Mss: N
Mail Queries: Y   Poetry Collections: Y

Jane Jordan Browne
Multimedia Product Development
410 S. Michigan Avenue, Rm. 724
Chicago, IL 60605
Phone: (312) 922-3063 Fax: (312) 922-1905

Contact: Jane Jordan Browne
Agency Commission: 15% U.S., 20% abroad
Manuscript categories represented:
  General nonfiction, mainstream fiction, genre fiction.
Agency accepts:
  Telephone Queries: N   Unsolicited Mss: N
          Mail Queries: Y   Poetry Collections: N

Knox Burger Associates, Ltd.

39½ Washington Square South
New York, NY 10012
Phone: (212) 533-2360 Fax: (212) 677-3170

Contact: Knox Burger
Agency Commission: 10% U.S., 19% abroad
Manuscript categories represented:
  Adult fiction and nonfiction. No science fiction, fan-
  tasy (anything to do with space), poetry. Accepts
  screenplays and short stories only from current
  clients.
Agency accepts:
  Telephone Queries: N   Unsolicited Mss: N
          Mail Queries: Y   Poetry Collections: N

Sheree Bykofsky Associates, Inc.

211 East 51st Street
Suite 11D
New York, NY 10022
Phone: (212) 308-1253

Contact: Sheree Bykofsky
Agency Commission: 10%

Manuscript categories represented:
Adult nonfiction and fiction. Specializes in popular nonfiction and reference.
Agency accepts:

Telephone Queries: N	Unsolicited Mss: N
Mail Queries: Y	Poetry Collections: N

Maria Carvainis Agency, Inc.
235 West End Avenue
New York, NY 10023
Phone: (212) 580-1559 Fax: (212) 877-3486

Contact: Maria Carvainis
Agency Commission: 15% U.S., 20% abroad
Manuscript categories represented:
Fiction: general, mainstream, contemporary women's, mystery, suspense, fantasy, historical, children's, and young adult. Nonfiction: business, finance, women's issues, biography, medicine.
Agency accepts:

Telephone Queries: Y	Unsolicited Mss: N
Mail Queries: Y	Poetry Collections: Y

Telephone queries accepted from published authors only. Poetry collections considered only from authors with poems published in national poetry magazines.

Martha Casselman, Literary Agent
P.O. Box 342
Calistoga, CA 94515-0342
Phone: (707) 942-4341

Contact: Martha Casselman
Agency Commission: 15%
Manuscript categories represented:

Fiction, nonfiction, and some children's books. Specialize in food books and cookbooks. "We regret we cannot return long-distance phone queries." Must say if multiple submission. No reading fee.

Agency accepts:

Telephone Queries: Y	Unsolicited Mss: N
Mail Queries: Y	Poetry Collections: N

The Catalog™ Literary Agency
Box 2964
Vancouver, WA 98668
Phone: (206) 694-8531

Contact: Douglas Storey
Agency Commission: 15% U.S., 20% abroad
Manuscript categories represented:

Popular professional books and textbooks in all subjects, mainstream fiction (no genre fiction). Specialize in business, health, money, science, technology, psychology, women's interests, how-to, and self-help. Query with an outline and sample chapters. Include a posted return mailer.

Agency accepts:

Telephone Queries: N	Unsolicited Mss: Y
Mail Queries: Y	Poetry Collections: N

No reading fee. If the project appears marketable, the writer will be offered an agreement. The agreement includes an up-front $250.00 fee that covers photocopying, postage, and telephone expenses.

The Linda Chester Literary Agency
265 Coast
La Jolla, CA 92037
Phone: (619) 454-3966 Fax: (619) 454-7338

Contact: Linda Chester, Laurie Fox
Agency Commission: 15% U.S., varies for sales abroad.
Manuscript categories represented:

Fiction, biography, health, psychology, popular culture, business, popular history, the arts (fine and performing). "We prefer literary fiction over commercial fiction, and unusual business books with fresh ideas." Will read unsolicited manuscripts, but prefer query first.

Agency accepts:

Telephone Queries: Y   Unsolicited Mss: Y
Mail Queries: Y   Poetry Collections: N

"We charge no fee for reading submissions. We do charge ($350) if an author asks for a written evaluation/critique of the work."

Faith Childs Literary Agency
275 West 96th Street
New York, NY 10025
Phone: (212) 662-1232 Fax: (212) 662-1456

Contact: Faith Hampton Childs
Agency Commission: 15% U.S., 20% abroad

Manuscript categories represented:
Literary fiction, narrative nonfiction. Specialize in history and current affairs, fiction, African-American issues.

Agency accepts:

Telephone Queries: N   Unsolicited Mss: N
Mail Queries: Y   Poetry Collections: N

Connie Clausen Associates
250 East 87th Street
New York, NY 10128
Phone: (212) 427-6135 Fax: (212) 996-7111

Contact: Connie Clausen, Andra Brill
Agency Commission: 15%
Manuscript categories represented:
Nonfiction only. Specialize in biographies, true crime, women's issues, health, beauty, essays, humor, how-to, true stories; feature movies and television films.

Agency accepts:

Telephone Queries: N   Unsolicited Mss: Y
Mail Queries: Y   Poetry Collections: N

Diane Cleaver, Inc.
Affil. with Greenburger Assoc.
55 Fifth Avenue, 15th floor
New York, NY 10003
Phone: (212) 206-5606 Fax: (212) 463-8718

Contact: Diane Cleaver
Agency Commission: 15%

Manuscript categories represented:
  Mainstream fiction, mystery and suspense (no science fiction). Nonfiction of all types except popular psychology and how-to. Prefer mail queries.
Agency accepts:
  Telephone Queries: Y   Unsolicited Mss: N
        Mail Queries: Y   Poetry Collections: N

Hy Cohen Literary Agency, Ltd.
111 West 57th Street
New York, NY 10019
Phone: (212) 757-5237

Contact: Hy Cohen
Agency Commission: 10% U.S., 20% abroad
Manuscript categories represented:
  Fiction and nonfiction. Will consider unsolicited manuscripts, but prefers to see first 100 pages.
Agency accepts:
  Telephone Queries: N   Unsolicited Mss: Y
        Mail Queries: Y   Poetry Collections: Y

Ruth Cohen, Inc., Literary Agency
P.O. Box 7626
Menlo Park, CA 94025
Phone: (415) 854-2054

Contact: Ruth Cohen
Agency Commission: 15%
Manuscript categories represented:
  Mysteries, women's fiction, juvenile fiction and nonfiction. Query with a letter and 10 opening pages.

Agency accepts:

Telephone Queries: Y   Unsolicited Mss: N

Mail Queries: Y   Poetry Collections: N

Collier Associates
2000 Flat Run Road
Seaman, OH 45679
Phone: (513) 764-1234

Contact: Oscar Collier
Agency Commission: 10%–15% U.S., 20% abroad
Manuscript categories represented:

Adult trade fiction and nonfiction. No textbooks or juveniles. Specialize in biography, autobiography of well-known individuals, U.S. history and current affairs, genre fiction. Prefer published authors who write well. Overloaded at present.

Agency accepts:

Telephone Queries: N   Unsolicited Mss: N

Mail Queries: Y   Poetry Collections: N

Frances Collin, Literary Agent
110 West 40th Street
New York, NY 10018
Phone: (212) 840-8664

Contact: Frances Collin
Agency Commission: 15%
Manuscript categories represented:

General trade fiction and nonfiction. Specialize in fantasy, mysteries, medical books, various environmental ("green") studies. Request an exclusive submission.

Agency accepts:

Telephone Queries: N	Unsolicited Mss: N
Mail Queries: Y	Poetry Collections: N

Don Congdon Associates, Inc. ————

156 Fifth Avenue
Suite 625
New York, NY 10010
Phone: (212) 645-1229 Fax: (212) 727-2688

Contact: Don Congdon, Michael Congdon, Susan Ramer
Agency Commission: 10% U.S., 19% abroad
Manuscript categories represented:
"Will consider any interesting trade book—fiction and nonfiction."

Agency accepts:

Telephone Queries: N	Unsolicited Mss: N
Mail Queries: Y	Poetry Collections: N

The Connor Literary Agency

640 West 153rd Street
New York, NY 10031
Phone: (212) 491-5233 Fax: (212) 491-5233

Contact: Marlene Connor
Agency Commission: 15%
Manuscript categories represented:
Mystery, horror, general nonfiction, women's fiction, children's literature, African-American fiction.

Agency accepts:
> Telephone Queries: N   Unsolicited Mss: N
>   Mail Queries: Y   Poetry Collections: N

"No reading fee for most manuscripts. Long novels may be sent to outside readers for $65 to $75, which includes a written critique."

Molly Malone Cook Literary Agency, Inc.
Box 338
Provincetown, MA 02657
Phone: (508) 487-1931

Contact: Molly Malone Cook
Agency Commission: 10%
Manuscript categories represented:
  Fiction, nonfiction.
Agency accepts:
> Telephone Queries: Y   Unsolicited Mss: N
>   Mail Queries: Y   Poetry Collections: N

The Doe Coover Agency
58 Sagamore Avenue
Medford, MA 02155
Phone: (617) 488-3937 Fax: (617) 488-3153

Contact: Doe Coover
Agency Commission: 15%
Manuscript categories represented:
  Nonfiction only: history, biography, social issues, cookbooks, women's issues.
Agency accepts:

Telephone Queries: Y   Unsolicited Mss: Y
Mail Queries: Y   Poetry Collections: N

Richard Curtis Associates, Inc.
171 East 74th Street
Suite 2
New York, NY 10021
Phone: (212) 772-7363 Fax: (212) 772-7393

Contact: Richard Curtis
Agency Commission: 15%
Manuscript categories represented:
   Fiction, nonfiction. Specialize in science fiction, action-adventure, romance.
Agency accepts:
   Telephone Queries: N   Unsolicited Mss: N
          Mail Queries: Y   Poetry Collections: N

Liz Darhansoff & Charles Verrill
1220 Park Avenue
New York, NY 10128
Phone: (212) 534-2479 Fax: (212) 996-1601

Contact: Leigh Feldman
Agency Commission: 10% U.S., 20% abroad, 15% film
Manuscript categories represented:
   Literary fiction, serious nonfiction.
Agency accepts:
   Telephone Queries: N   Unsolicited Mss: N
          Mail Queries: Y   Poetry Collections: N

Joan Daves Agency
21 West 26th Street
New York, NY 10010-1003
Phone: (212) 685-2663 Fax: (212) 685-1781

Contact: Jennifer Lyons
Agency Commission: 15%–20%
Manuscript categories represented:
Fiction, nonfiction, poetry, literature.
Agency accepts:

Telephone Queries: N	Unsolicited Mss: Y
Mail Queries: Y	Poetry Collections: Y

Elaine Davie Literary Agency
Village Gate Square
274 North Goodman Street
Rochester, NY 14607
Phone: (716) 442-0830 Fax: (716) 442-2870

Contact: Elaine Davie
Agency Commission: 15%
Manuscript categories represented:
Popular and commercial fiction and nonfiction, particularly books by and for women. Specialize in romance fiction: traditional, contemporary, historical.
Agency accepts:

Telephone Queries: N	Unsolicited Mss: N
Mail Queries: Y	Poetry Collections: N

"We pride ourselves on the fact that we never charge a fee of any kind."

Anita Diamant
Subs. of The Writers Workshop, Inc.
310 Madison Avenue
New York, NY 10017
Phone: (212) 687-1122

Contact: Anita Diamant
Agency Commission: 15% U.S., 20% abroad
Manuscript categories represented:
  Fiction, nonfiction, and young adult. Specialize in
  adult fiction.
Agency accepts:
  Telephone Queries: Y   Unsolicited Mss: N
      Mail Queries: Y   Poetry Collections: N

Janet Dight Literary Agency
3075 Inspiration Drive
Colorado Springs, CO 90817
Phone: (719) 597-7675

Contact: Janet Dight
Agency Commission: 15% books, film, television; 20%
  abroad
Manuscript categories represented:
  Adult and juvenile fiction and nonfiction.
Agency accepts:
  Telephone Queries: N   Unsolicited Mss: N
      Mail Queries: Y   Poetry Collections: N

Sandra Dijkstra Literary Agency
1155 Camino del Mar
Suite 515
Del Mar, CA 92014
Phone: (619) 755-3115 Fax: (619) 792-1494

Contact: Katherine Goodwin, Rita Holm
Agency Commission: 15%
Manuscript categories represented:
  Fiction: specialize in contemporary, literary, mystery/
  thriller, mainstream; also represent science fiction/
  fantasy, historical romance. Nonfiction: science,
  health, history, biography, psychology and self-help,
  memoir, current affairs, business, true crime.
Agency accepts:

Telephone Queries: N	Unsolicited Mss: Y
Mail Queries: Y	Poetry Collections: N

The Jonathan Dolger Agency
49 East 96th Street
Suite 9B
New York, NY 10128
Phone: (212) 427-1853 Fax: (212) 369-7118

Contact: Carol-Ann Dearnaley
Agency Commission: 15%
Manuscript categories represented:
  Adult trade fiction and nonfiction, illustrated books.
Agency accepts:

Telephone Queries: N	Unsolicited Mss: N
Mail Queries: Y	Poetry Collections: N

Donadio & Ashworth, Inc., Literary Representatives
231 West 22nd Street
New York, NY 10011
Phone: (212) 691-8077 Fax: (212) 633-2837

Contact: Neil Olson
Agency Commission: 10%
Manuscript categories represented:
  Mainstream fiction and nonfiction. No genre fiction.
  Send 50 pages of manuscript with query.
Agency accepts:
  Telephone Queries: N   Unsolicited Mss: Y
         Mail Queries: Y   Poetry Collections: N

Thomas C. Donlan
143 East 43rd Street
New York, NY 10017-4007
Phone: (212) 697-1629

Contact: Thomas C. Donlan
Agency Commission: 10%
Manuscript categories represented:
  Strictly limited to Catholic philosophy and theology.
  "Always query first; absolutely no unsolicited man-
  uscripts read; absolutely no telephone queries
  accepted."
Agency accepts:
  Telephone Queries: N   Unsolicited Mss: N
         Mail Queries: Y   Poetry Collections: N

Dupree/Miller & Associates, Inc.
5518 Dyer Street
Suite 3
Dallas, TX 75206
Phone: (214) 692-1388 Fax: (214) 987-9654

Contact: David Smith
Agency Commission: 15%
Manuscript categories represented:
  Nonfiction or fiction: full-length works, any subject;
  no children's literature, short story collections, or po-
  etry. "As an agency we have to be concerned with
  the bottom line—a book's marketability; we're not
  an editorial review service."
Agency accepts:
  Telephone Queries: N   Unsolicited Mss: Y
        Mail Queries: Y   Poetry Collections: N

Unsolicited manuscripts will be read when accompanied
by a $10 handling fee.

Ethan Ellenberg, Literary Agent
548 Broadway
Suite 5-E
New York, NY 10012
Phone: (212) 431-4554 Fax: (212) 941-4652

Contact: Ethan Ellenberg
Agency Commission: 15%
Manuscript categories represented:
  All, but specialize in commercial and literary fiction
  of all genres, including mystery, thriller, science fic-

tion, fantasy, horror, women's, military, etc.; quality nonfiction. No poetry.
Agency accepts:
Telephone Queries: Y   Unsolicited Mss: Y
       Mail Queries: Y   Poetry Collections: N

Nicholas Ellison, Inc.
Affil. with Greenburger Assoc.
55 Fifth Avenue, 15th floor
New York, NY 10003
Phone: (212) 206-6050 Fax: (212) 463-8718

Contact: Jennifer Reavis
Agency Commission: 15%
Manuscript categories represented:
Fiction and nonfiction; no children's books, short story collections, or screenplays.
Agency accepts:
Telephone Queries: N   Unsolicited Mss: N
       Mail Queries: Y   Poetry Collections: N

Ann Elmo Agency, Inc.
60 East 42nd Street
New York, NY 10165
Phone: (212) 661-2880, 81 Fax: (212) 661-2883

Contact: Lettie Lee
Agency Commission: 15% U.S., 20% abroad
Manuscript categories represented:
Fiction, nonfiction, juvenile.
Agency accepts:

Telephone Queries: Y   Unsolicited Mss: N
Mail Queries: Y   Poetry Collections: N

Felicia Eth Literary Representation

555 Bryant Street
Suite 350
Palo Alto, CA 94301
Phone: (415) 375-1276 Fax: (415) 375-1277

Contact: Felicia Eth
Agency Commission: 15%
Manuscript categories represented:

Very selectively—mainstream literary fiction, primarily contemporary, psychological; intelligent, thoughtful nonfiction; journalistic investigation, psychological literature, health, women's issues, contemporary affairs. "Wide-ranging interests difficult to categorize."

Agency accepts:

Telephone Queries: Y   Unsolicited Mss: Y
Mail Queries: Y   Poetry Collections: N

Farber & Freeman

14 East 75th Street
New York, NY 10021
Phone: (212) 861-7075 Fax: (212) 687-0056

Contact: Anne Farber, Sandra Freeman
Agency Commission: 10%–15%
Manuscript categories represented:

Fiction, nonfiction, plays—no short stories.

Agency accepts:

Telephone Queries: Y   Unsolicited Mss: Y
Mail Queries: Y   Poetry Collections: N

John Farquharson, Ltd.
250 West 57th Street
New York, NY 10107
Phone: (212) 245-1993

Contact: Jane Gelfman, Deborah Schneider
Agency Commission: 10% U.S., 20% abroad
Manuscript categories represented:
General fiction and nonfiction: literary, mainstream,
mysteries. No genre romances, Westerns, science fic-
tion, children's books, poetry.
Agency accepts:
Telephone Queries: N   Unsolicited Mss: N
Mail Queries: Y   Poetry Collections: N

Marje Fields
165 West 46th Street
Suite 1205
New York, NY 10036
Phone: (212) 764-5740

Contact: Ray Powers
Agency Commission: 15%
Manuscript categories represented:
Fiction and nonfiction. No short stories. Specialize in
novels, particularly by new writers.
Agency accepts:

Telephone Queries: N   Unsolicited Mss: N
Mail Queries: Y   Poetry Collections: N

Flannery, White & Stone, A Writer's Agency
180 Cook
Suite 404
Denver, CO 80206
Phone: (303) 399-2264 Fax: (303) 399-3006

Contact: Connie Solowiej
Agency Commission: 10% screenplays, 15% all other
Manuscript categories represented:
  Screenplays, unique nonfiction, mainstream and literary fiction, true crime, children's books. Mail query with sample chapter.
Agency accepts:
  Telephone Queries: Y   Unsolicited Mss: N
  Mail Queries: Y   Poetry Collections: N

"No reading fee; evaluation fee may be charged if author wants a critique—this is negotiable."

Candice Fuhrman Literary Agency
30 Ramona Road
Forest Knolls, CA 94933
Phone: (415) 488-0161

Contact: Candice Fuhrman
Agency Commission: 15%
Manuscript categories represented:
  Adult nonfiction and fiction. No genre fiction, poetry, or children's literature.

Agency accepts:
Telephone Queries: N   Unsolicited Mss: Y
Mail Queries: Y   Poetry Collections: N

Jay Garon-Brooke Associates

415 Central Park West
New York, NY 10025
Phone: (212) 866-3654 Fax: (212) 666-6016

Contact: Jay Garon, Jean Free
Agency Commission: 15% U.S., 30% abroad
Manuscript categories represented:
"Mainly mainstream novels and popular nonfiction."
Agency accepts:
Telephone Queries: N   Unsolicited Mss: N
Mail Queries: Y   Poetry Collections: N

Max Gartenberg, Literary Agent

521 Fifth Avenue
Suite 1700
New York, NY 10175
Phone: (212) 860-8451 Fax: (201) 535-5033

Contact: Max Gartenberg
Agency Commission: 10% U.S. and Canada, 15% elsewhere
Manuscript categories represented:
General nonfiction and fiction of book length.
Agency accepts:
Telephone Queries: N   Unsolicited Mss: N
Mail Queries: Y   Poetry Collections: N

Rene Wayne Golden
8983 Norma Place
West Hollywood, CA 90069
Phone: (213) 550-8232 Fax: (213) 276-7736

Contact: Rene Wayne Golden
Agency Commission: 15%
Manuscript categories represented:
  Nonfiction, especially natural history, biography, politics. Also represents some fiction. "I'm a lawyer with a literary practice." Manuscripts turned down for representation will be critiqued for a fee, only if the author desires.
Agency accepts:
  Telephone Queries: N   Unsolicited Mss: N
         Mail Queries: Y   Poetry Collections: N

Goldfarb, Kaufman & O'Toole
918 16th Street, N.W.
Suite 503
Washington, DC 20006
Phone: (202) 466-3030 Fax: (202) 293-3187

Contact: Nina Graybill, Ronald Goldfarb
Agency Commission: 15%
Manuscript categories represented:
  Fiction and nonfiction.
Agency accepts:
  Telephone Queries: Y   Unsolicited Mss: N
         Mail Queries: Y   Poetry Collections: Y

"No fee charged, but we accept manuscripts on an exclusive basis only because of this. Generally we ask for a synopsis, several chapters, and some biographical material from the author."

Goodman Associates
500 West End Avenue
New York, NY 10024
Phone: (212) 873-4806 Fax: (212) 580-3278

Contact: Elise Simon Goodman
Agency Commission: 15% U.S., 20% abroad
Manuscript categories represented:
Adult fiction and nonfiction. Specialize in literary fiction, work by journalists, cookbooks, biographies, thrillers.
Agency accepts:

Telephone Queries: N	Unsolicited Mss: Y
Mail Queries: Y	Poetry Collections: N

Charlotte Gordon
235 East 22nd Street
New York, NY 10010
Phone: (212) 679-5363

Contact: Charlotte Gordon
Agency Commission: 15%
Manuscript categories represented:
Adult fiction and nonfiction, some juvenile. "An eclectic mix: what we like, we'll represent (if we think it has a chance in today's difficult market). No unsolicited manuscripts. I will read query letters that

include 5 pages of the manuscript and a very brief plot outline—no fee."

Agency accepts:

Telephone Queries: N	Unsolicited Mss: N
Mail Queries: Y	Poetry Collections: N

Critical evaluation is a separate category: fees vary and are negotiable. "If I ask to see a manuscript, no charge for reading. I will work with writers whose work seems to have promise, but if I don't want to represent a manuscript, it doesn't mean it's not good."

Gotham Art & Literary Agency

1133 Broadway
Suite 924
New York, NY 10010
Phone: (212) 989-2737 Fax: (212) 645-7731

Contact: Anne Elisabeth Suter
Agency Commission: 15% U.S., 20% abroad
Manuscript categories represented:
   Specialize in fiction, art, children's books. Represent some nonfiction.
Agency accepts:

Telephone Queries: N	Unsolicited Mss: N
Mail Queries: Y	Poetry Collections: N

Sanford J. Greenburger Associates, Inc.

55 Fifth Avenue, 15th floor
New York, NY 10003
Phone: (212) 206-5600 Fax: (212) 463-8718

Contact: Heide Lange, Faith Hamlin, Beth Vesel
Agency Commission: 15%
Manuscript categories represented:
Fiction and nonfiction.
Agency accepts:
Telephone Queries: Y   Unsolicited Mss: N
Mail Queries: Y   Poetry Collections: N

Maia Gregory Associates

311 East 72nd Street
New York, NY 10021
Phone: (212) 288-0310

Contact: Maia Gregory
Agency Commission: 10%
Manuscript categories represented:
Nonfiction, biography, art books; no first novels. Include short outline with query.
Agency accepts:
Telephone Queries: Y   Unsolicited Mss: N
Mail Queries: Y   Poetry Collections: N

Lew Grimes Literary Agency

250 West 54th Street
Suite 800
New York, NY 10019-5586
Phone: (212) 974-9505 Fax: (212) 974-9525

Contact: Lew Grimes
Agency Commission: 15% U.S., 20% abroad
Manuscript categories represented:
Specialize in general interest or literary nonfiction,

literary or genre fiction; illustrated books, film and television scripts.

Agency accepts:

Telephone Queries: N   Unsolicited Mss: Y
Mail Queries: Y   Poetry Collections: Y

Will read unsolicited manuscripts; enclose $10 postage and handling charge with manuscript.

Maxine Groffsky Literary Agency
2 Fifth Avenue
New York, NY 10011
Phone: (212) 473-0004 Fax: (212) 982-4143

Contact: Maxine Groffsky
Agency Commission: 15%
Manuscript categories represented:
  Fiction and nonfiction. Specialize in literary fiction.
Agency accepts:

Telephone Queries: Y   Unsolicited Mss: Y
Mail Queries: Y   Poetry Collections: N

The Charlotte Gusay Literary Agency
10532 Blythe Avenue
Los Angeles, CA 90064
Phone: (213) 559-0831 Fax: (212) 559-2639

Contact: Charlotte Gusay
Agency Commission: 15% book sales, 10% dramatic/
  film sales
Manuscript categories represented:
  Specialize in fiction (especially literary), strong and

unusual nonfiction, nonsexist and literary children's projects. Also represent books to film, screenplays, selected children's books. No poetry or short story collections, horror or science fiction; no magazine articles.

Agency accepts:

Telephone Queries: N   Unsolicited Mss: N
Mail Queries: Y   Poetry Collections: N

Jeanne K. Hanson Literary Agency

5111 Wooddale Avenue South
Edina, MN 55424
Phone: (612) 922-9471 Fax: (612) 922-9041

Contact: Jeanne Hanson
Agency Commission: 15%
Manuscript categories represented:
Nonfiction; books written by journalists.

Agency accepts:

Telephone Queries: Y   Unsolicited Mss: N
Mail Queries: Y   Poetry Collections: N

John Hawkins & Associates, Inc.

71 West 23rd Street
Suite 1600
New York, NY 10010
Phone: (212) 807-7040 Fax: (212) 807-9555

Contact: William Reiss, John Hawkins, Sharon Friedman
Agency Commission: not specified
Manuscript categories represented:

"Most manuscript categories represented, other than poetry and plays."
Agency accepts:

Telephone Queries: Y	Unsolicited Mss: Y
Mail Queries: Y	Poetry Collections: N

The Jeff Herman Agency, Inc.
500 Greenwich Street
Suite 501-C
New York, NY 10013
Phone: (212) 941-0540

Contact: Jeff Herman
Agency Commission: 15%
Manuscript categories represented:
  Primarily nonfiction; open to all areas.
Agency accepts:

Telephone Queries: N	Unsolicited Mss: N
Mail Queries: Y	Poetry Collections: N

Susan Herner Rights Agency, Inc.
110 West 40th Street
Suite 1403
New York, NY 10018
Phone: (212) 221-7515 Fax: (212) 221-7517

Contact: Susan Herner
Agency Commission: 15% U.S.
Manuscript categories represented:
  Adult fiction and nonfiction: commercial and literary.
Agency accepts:

Telephone Queries: Y   Unsolicited Mss: N
Mail Queries: Y   Poetry Collections: N

Frederick Hill Associates
1842 Union Street
San Francisco, CA 94123
Phone: (415) 921-2910 Fax: (415) 921-2802

Contact: Bonnie Nadell, Frederick Hill
Agency Commission: 15% U.S., 20% abroad, 15%
  dramatic
Manuscript categories represented:
  Fiction and general nonfiction, literary short stories,
  young adult fiction and nonfiction, cookbooks.
Agency accepts:
  Telephone Queries: Y   Unsolicited Mss: N
  Mail Queries: Y   Poetry Collections: N

John L. Hochmann Books
320 East 58th Street
New York, NY 10022
Phone: (212) 519-0505 Fax: (212) 421-8699

Contact: John L. Hochmann
Agency Commission: 15% of author's gross receipts
Manuscript categories represented:
  Biography, current affairs, college textbooks, enter-
  tainment, social history, food and nutrition. Send de-
  tailed outlines. Include qualifications for writing book
  and comparisons with other books on same subject.
Agency accepts:

Telephone Queries: N   Unsolicited Mss: N
Mail Queries: Y   Poetry Collections: N

Hull House Literary Agency

240 East 82nd Street
New York, NY 10028
Phone: (212) 988-0725 Fax: (212) 794-8758

Contact: Lydia Mortimer
Agency Commission: 15% U.S.
Manuscript categories represented:
  Commercial fiction and nonfiction. Specialize in crime/suspense novels, true crime nonfiction, military history of general interest.
Agency accepts:
  Telephone Queries: N   Unsolicited Mss: N
  Mail Queries: Y   Poetry Collections: N

Independent Publishers Services
The Gottstein Company

Box 135
Volcano, CA 95689
Phone: (209) 296-7989 Fax: (209) 296-4515

Contact: Ruth Gottstein
Agency Commission: not specified
Manuscript categories represented:
  Nonfiction: women's issues, children's social issues.
Agency accepts:
  Telephone Queries: N   Unsolicited Mss: N
  Mail Queries: Y   Poetry Collections: N

International Creative Management
40 West 57th Street
New York, NY 10019
Phone: (212) 556-5600 Fax: (212) 556-5665

Contact: not specified
Agency Commission: not specified
Manuscript categories represented:
   Nine agents in the literary department see all queries;
   send query letter with one sample chapter.
Agency accepts:
   Telephone Queries: N   Unsolicited Mss: N
            Mail Queries: Y   Poetry Collections: N

International Publisher Associates, Inc.
746 West Shore
Sparta, NJ 07871
Phone: (201) 729-9321

Contact: Joe DeRogatis
Agency Commission: 15% U.S., 20% abroad
Manuscript categories represented:
   Any nonfiction.
Agency accepts:
   Telephone Queries: N   Unsolicited Mss: N
            Mail Queries: Y   Poetry Collections: N

Melanie Jackson Agency
250 West 57th Street
Suite 1119
New York, NY 10107-1119
Phone: (212) 582-8585 Fax: (212) 586-0427

Contact: Melanie Jackson, Miranda Field
Agency Commission: not specified
Manuscript categories represented:
"Always query first; no unsolicited manuscripts read."
Agency accepts:

Telephone Queries: N	Unsolicited Mss: N
Mail Queries: Y	Poetry Collections: N

Sharon Jarvis & Co.
260 Willard Avenue
Staten Island, NY 10314
Phone: (718) 720-2120

Contact: Sharon Jarvis, Joan Winston
Agency Commission: 15%
Manuscript categories represented:
Specialize in occult nonfiction. Also represent genre fiction and popular nonfiction. No short fiction or nonfiction; no scripts, poetry, or children's literature. "We don't look at any manuscripts unless they come via a source known to us."
Agency accepts:

Telephone Queries: N	Unsolicited Mss: N
Mail Queries: Y	Poetry Collections: N

Unpublished writers are referred to recommended freelance editors.

JCA Literary Agency
27 West 20th Street
Suite 1103
New York, NY 10011
Phone: (212) 807-0888 Fax: (212) 807-0461

Contact: Jane Cushman, Jeff Gerecke
Agency Commission: 10% U.S., 20% abroad
Manuscript categories represented:
Mainstream fiction and nonfiction; no self-help or how-to; no juvenile, science fiction, romances, or cookbooks. Specialize in current affairs, history, biography, true crime; in fiction, crime and mysteries, political and/or military thrillers, top-quality women's fiction, literary fiction.
Agency accepts:

Telephone Queries: N	Unsolicited Mss: N
Mail Queries: Y	Poetry Collections: N

JLM Literary Agents
17221 East 17th
Suite L
Santa Ana, CA 92701
Phone: (714) 547-4870 Fax: (714) 547-1807

Contact: Judy Semler
Agency Commission: 15%
Manuscript categories represented:
Primarily nonfiction: good women's self-help, popular science, psychology, environmental. Very few

novels—some women's literary fiction, mostly mystery. Query first.
Agency accepts:

Telephone Queries: N	Unsolicited Mss: N
Mail Queries: Y	Poetry Collections: N

No reading fee, but an unpublished author may be required to pay a $100 "contract fee" to offset initial marketing costs.

The Lloyd Jones Literary Agency
4301 Hidden Creek
Arlington, TX 76016
Phone: (817) 483-5103 Fax: (817) 483-8791

Contact: Lloyd Jones
Agency Commission: 15%
Manuscript categories represented:
True crime, business, mystery, romance, self-help. Specialize in business and self-help.
Agency accepts:

Telephone Queries: N	Unsolicited Mss: Y
Mail Queries: Y	Poetry Collections: N

"We do not charge for any service."

Louise B. Ketz Agency
1485 First Avenue
Suite 4B
New York, NY 10021
Phone: (212) 535-9259

Contact: Louise B. Ketz
Agency Commission: 10%–15%
Manuscript categories represented:
Science, sports, business, history, biography, reference.
Agency accepts:
Telephone Queries: Y   Unsolicited Mss: N
Mail Queries: Y   Poetry Collections: N

Virginia Kidd, Literary Agent
538 East Harford Street
P.O. Box 278
Milford, PA 18337
Phone: (717) 296-6205 Fax: (717) 296-7266

Contact: Virginia Kidd
Agency Commission: 10% U.S., 20% abroad and film
Manuscript categories represented:
All kinds of fiction; not much nonfiction. Specialize in speculative fiction. "I am not looking for new clients. My lists are full."
Agency accepts:
Telephone Queries: N   Unsolicited Mss: N
Mail Queries: Y   Poetry Collections: N

Kidde, Hoyt & Picard
335 East 51st Street
New York, NY 10022
Phone: (212) 755-9461

Contact: Katharine Kidde
Agency Commission: 10%

Manuscript categories represented:
Fiction: romance, mainstream, and literary. General nonfiction.
Agency accepts:

Telephone Queries: Y	Unsolicited Mss: N
Mail Queries: Y	Poetry Collections: N

Kirchoff/Wohlberg, Inc.
866 United Nations Plaza
Suite 525
New York, NY 10017
Phone: (212) 644-2020 Fax: (212) 223-4387

Contact: Elizabeth Pulitzer, John R. Whitman
Agency Commission: Varies
Manuscript categories represented:
Children's and young adult manuscripts only. Agency commission depends upon whether the children's book author is also illustrating the book.
Agency accepts:

Telephone Queries: N	Unsolicited Mss: Y
Mail Queries: Y	Poetry Collections: Y

Harvey Klinger, Inc.
301 West 53rd Street
New York, NY 10019
Phone: (212) 581-7068 Fax: (212) 315-3823

Contact: Harvey Klinger
Agency Commission: 15% U.S., 25% abroad
Manuscript categories represented:

Fiction: literary and commercial. Nonfiction: psychology, health, biography, true crime, how-to.
Agency accepts:

Telephone Queries: N	Unsolicited Mss: Y
Mail Queries: Y	Poetry Collections: N

Barbara S. Kouts
P.O. Box 558
Bellport, NY 11713
Phone: (516) 286-1278 Fax: (516) 286-1538

Contact: Barbara S. Kouts
Agency Commission: 10%
Manuscript categories represented:
Specialize in literary fiction and children's books. Also represent adult fiction and nonfiction.
Agency accepts:

Telephone Queries: N	Unsolicited Mss: N
Mail Queries: Y	Poetry Collections: N

Sidney B. Kramer
Mews Books, Ltd.
20 Bluewater Hill
Westport, CT 06880
Phone: (203) 227-1836 Fax: (203) 227-1144

Contact: Sidney B. Kramer, Pres.
Agency Commission: 15% U.S., 20% abroad
Manuscript categories represented:
50% juvenile, 50% miscellaneous. No plays or short story collections.
Agency accepts:

Telephone Queries: N	Unsolicited Mss: Y
Mail Queries: Y	Poetry Collections: N

"We do ask $350 against commissions toward marketing and other office costs."

Edite Kroll Literary Agency
12 Grayhurst Park
Portland, ME 04102
Phone: (207) 773-4922 Fax: (207) 773-3936

Contact: Edite Kroll
Agency Commission: 15% U.S., 20%–25% abroad, 15% film, dramatic
Manuscript categories represented:
  Adult fiction and issue-oriented nonfiction; feminist trade books; humor; children's picture books by artists who write and illustrate their own books; children's fiction.
Agency accepts:

Telephone Queries: N	Unsolicited Mss: N
Mail Queries: Y	Poetry Collections: N

Peter Lampack Agency, Inc.
551 Fifth Avenue
Suite 2015
New York, NY 10017
Phone: (212) 687-9106 Fax: (212) 687-9109

Contact: Peter Lampack
Agency Commission: 15% U.S., 20% abroad
Manuscript categories represented:

Commercial and literary fiction. Specialize in non-fiction written by an expert in a given field, male-oriented thrillers, female-oriented contemporary fiction, mysteries, psychological horror, literary fiction that involves a major social issue.
Agency accepts:
Telephone Queries: N   Unsolicited Mss: N
Mail Queries: Y   Poetry Collections: N

The Robert Lantz-Joy Harris Literary Agency
888 Seventh Avenue, 25th floor
New York, NY 10106
Phone: (212) 262-8177 Fax: (212) 262-8707

Contact: Joy Harris
Agency Commission: 15%
Manuscript categories represented:
Mysteries, thrillers, literary fiction, serious nonfiction.
Agency accepts:
Telephone Queries: N   Unsolicited Mss: N
Mail Queries: Y   Poetry Collections: N

Michael Larsen/Elizabeth Pomada
1029 Jones Street
San Francisco, CA 94109
Phone: (415) 673-0939

Contact: Mike Larsen, Elizabeth Pomada
Agency Commission: 15% U.S., 20% abroad
Manuscript categories represented:
Fiction and nonfiction for adults: commercial and lit-

erary fiction; popular psychology, business, science, health, humor, art books, biography, popular culture. Mike Larsen for nonfiction; Elizabeth Pomada for fiction.

Agency accepts:

Telephone Queries: Y	Unsolicited Mss: N
Mail Queries: Y	Poetry Collections: N

The M. Sue Lasbury Literary Agency
4861 Ocean Boulevard
San Diego, CA 92109
Phone: (619) 483-7170 Fax: (619) 483-1853

Contact: Sue Lasbury, John Cochran
Agency Commission: 15% U.S., 20% abroad
Manuscript categories represented:

Fiction: mystery, mainstream, literary. All areas of nonfiction: author must be an authority in the field. "Seventy-five percent of our work is in the area of nonfiction. We enjoy working with academics who want to write for the general book market and can make their writing accessible."

Agency accepts:

Telephone Queries: Y	Unsolicited Mss: N
Mail Queries: Y	Poetry Collections: N

The Maureen Lasher Agency
P.O. Box 888
Pacific Palisades, CA 90272
Phone: (213) 459-8415 Fax: (213) 459-9659

Contact: Ann Cashman

Agency Commission: 15%
Manuscript categories represented:
Fiction, nonfiction.
Agency accepts:
Telephone Queries: N   Unsolicited Mss: Y
Mail Queries: Y   Poetry Collections: N

The Lazear Agency, Inc.
430 First Avenue North
Suite 416
Minneapolis, MN 55401
Phone: (612) 332-8640 Fax: (612) 332-4648

Contact: Wendy Lazear
Agency Commission: 15%
Manuscript categories represented:
Mainstream adult and young adult fiction; mass market nonfiction.
Agency accepts:
Telephone Queries: Y   Unsolicited Mss: N
Mail Queries: Y   Poetry Collections: N

The Adele Leone Agency, Inc.
26 Nantucket Place
Scarsdale, NY 10583
Phone: (914) 961-2965 Fax: (914) 337-0361

Contact: Adele Leone
Agency Commission: 15%
Manuscript categories represented:
Mainstream fiction; nonfiction (self-help, science, nutrition, health, new age). Specialize in women's fic-

tion, science fiction, fantasy, horror, Westerns, hard science, health.

Agency accepts:

Telephone Queries: Y	Unsolicited Mss: Y
Mail Queries: Y	Poetry Collections: N

Lescher & Lescher, Ltd.

67 Irving Place
New York, NY 10003
Phone: (212) 529-1790 Fax: (212) 529-2719

Contact: Robert Lescher, Susan Lescher
Agency Commission: 15%
Manuscript categories represented:
Fiction, nonfiction (biography, contemporary affairs, food and wine).

Agency accepts:

Telephone Queries: N	Unsolicited Mss: N
Mail Queries: Y	Poetry Collections: N

Levant & Wales, Inc.

108 Hayes Street
Seattle, WA 98109
Phone: (206) 284-7114 Fax: (206) 286-1025

Contact: Elizabeth Wales
Agency Commission: 15% U.S.
Manuscript categories represented:
Quality mainstream fiction and nonfiction. For submissions, please send a query letter and writing excerpt with an SASE. The agency will respond as soon

as possible to queries and within four weeks to manuscripts sent at the request of the agency.
Agency accepts:

Telephone Queries: Y	Unsolicited Mss: N
Mail Queries: Y	Poetry Collections: N

Ellen Levine Literary Agency, Inc.
15 East 26th Street
Suite 1801
New York, NY 10010
Phone: (212) 889-0620 Fax: (212) 725-4501

Contact: Ellen Levine, Diana Finch, Anne Dubuisson
Agency Commission: 10%–20%
Manuscript categories represented:
Specialize in literary fiction, biography, books by journalists, women's issues, science, history, psychology, cultural issues, politics. Short stories and articles by established clients only.
Agency accepts:

Telephone Queries: N	Unsolicited Mss: N
Mail Queries: Y	Poetry Collections: N

Ray Lincoln Literary Agency
Elkins Park House
Suite 107-B
Elkins Park, PA 19117
Phone: (215) 635-0827

Contact: (Mrs.) Ray Lincoln
Agency Commission: 15% U.S., 20% abroad
Manuscript categories represented:

All types of adult and children's fiction and nonfiction. "I look for fine novels, biographies, works on nature and science and the world around us, including child-rearing and family matters, social responsibility, etc."

Agency accepts:

Telephone Queries: Y	Unsolicited Mss: N
Mail Queries: Y	Poetry Collections: N

Literary & Creative Artists Agency
3539 Albemarle Street, N.W.
Washington, DC 20008
Phone: (202) 362-4688 Fax: (202) 362-4688

Contact: Muriel G. Nellis, Jane F. Roberts
Agency Commission: 15%
Manuscript categories represented:
Broad range of fiction and nonfiction, including biography, politics, public affairs, health, true accounts of human drama/experience, cooking, business; also theatrical and screenplays.

Agency accepts:

Telephone Queries: N	Unsolicited Mss: N
Mail Queries: Y	Poetry Collections: N

Nancy Love Literary Agency
250 East 65th Street
New York, NY 10021
Phone: (212) 980-3499 Fax: (212) 308-6405

Contact: Nancy Love
Agency Commission: 15%

Manuscript categories represented:
In nonfiction, specialize in current events, true crime, health, parenting, celebrities, reference. No technical or academic. In fiction, mystery, thrillers, break-out mainstream. No romance or science fiction.
Agency accepts:
Telephone Queries: Y   Unsolicited Mss: Y
Mail Queries: Y   Poetry Collections: N

Donald MacCampbell, Inc.
12 East 41st Street
New York, NY 10017
Phone: (212) 683-5580

Contact: Maureen Moran
Agency Commission: 10%, 15% on first novels, 20% translation
Manuscript categories represented:
Novels, especially popular categories (except science fiction and horror). Specialize in novels for women's market. Prefer mail queries.
Agency accepts:
Telephone Queries: Y   Unsolicited Mss: N
Mail Queries: Y   Poetry Collections: N

Carol Mann Agency
55 Fifth Avenue
New York, NY 10003
Phone: (212) 206-5635 Fax: (212) 463-8718

Contact: Carol Mann
Agency Commission: 15%

Manuscript categories represented:
History, biography, psychology, social sciences, popular culture. Telephone queries from published authors only.
Agency accepts:

Telephone Queries: Y	Unsolicited Mss: N
Mail Queries: Y	Poetry Collections: N

March Tenth, Inc.
4 Myrtle Street
Haworth, NJ 07641
Phone: (201) 387-6551 Fax: (201) 387-6552

Contact: Sandra Choron
Agency Commission: 15%
Manuscript categories represented:
Nonfiction only: general nonfiction, popular culture.
Agency accepts:

Telephone Queries: Y	Unsolicited Mss: Y
Mail Queries: Y	Poetry Collections: N

Barbara Markowitz
117 North Mansfield Avenue
Los Angeles, CA 90036
Phone: (213) 939-5927

Contact: Barbara Markowitz, Judith Rosenthal
Agency Commission: 15%
Manuscript categories represented:
Fiction and nonfiction for adults and children (mid-level, 8–12 years). No activity books, verse, poetry, or illustrated books. Specialize in murder mysteries

for adults, fiction and nonfiction for children, biographies, historical fiction.
Agency accepts:

Telephone Queries: Y	Unsolicited Mss: N
Mail Queries: Y	Poetry Collections: N

Mildred Marmur Associates, Ltd.
310 Madison Avenue
Suite 607
New York, NY 10017
Phone: (212) 949-6055 Fax: (212) 687-6894

Contact: Mildred Marmur
Agency Commission: 15%
Manuscript categories represented:
Serious nonfiction, including science, politics, history, literary biography, and cookbooks. Literary and commercial fiction.
Agency accepts:

Telephone Queries: N	Unsolicited Mss: N
Mail Queries: Y	Poetry Collections: N

Jed Mattes, Inc.
175 West 73rd Street
Suite 8H
New York, NY 10023
Phone: (212) 580-8009 Fax: (212) 595-9306

Contact: Jed Mattes
Agency Commission: 15% U.S., 20% abroad
Manuscript categories represented:

Fiction and nonfiction. No poetry or juvenile. Specialize in mystery and gay issues.
Agency accepts:
Telephone Queries: N   Unsolicited Mss: N
Mail Queries: Y   Poetry Collections: N

Margret McBride Literary Agency
4350 Executive Drive
Suite 225
San Diego, CA 92121
Phone: (619) 457-0550 Fax: (619) 457-2315

Contact: Winifred Golden, Susan Travis
Agency Commission: 15% U.S., 25% abroad
Manuscript categories represented:
Mainstream fiction and nonfiction.
Agency accepts:
Telephone Queries: N   Unsolicited Mss: N
Mail Queries: Y   Poetry Collections: N

Anita D. McClellan Associates
50 Stearns Street
Cambridge, MA 02138
Phone: (617) 864-3448

Contact: Anita D. McClellan
Agency Commission: 15%
Manuscript categories represented:
General trade adult fiction and nonfiction; scholarly nonfiction.
Agency accepts:

Telephone Queries: N   Unsolicited Mss: N
Mail Queries: Y   Poetry Collections: N

McIntosh & Otis, Inc.
310 Madison Avenue
Suite 607
New York, NY 10017
Phone: (212) 687-7400 Fax: (212) 687-6894

Contact: Julie Fallowfield, Dorothy Markinko, Eugene
  Winick
Agency Commission: not specified
Manuscript categories represented:
  Adult and juvenile literary fiction and nonfiction.
Agency accepts:
  Telephone Queries: N   Unsolicited Mss: N
  Mail Queries: Y   Poetry Collections: N

Helen Merrill, Ltd.
435 West 23rd Street
Suite 1A
New York, NY 10011
Phone: (212) 691-5326

Contact: Helen Merrill
Agency Commission: 10%
Manuscript categories represented:
  Nonfiction and fiction, including genre fiction. No
  poetry.
Agency accepts:

Telephone Queries: N   Unsolicited Mss: N
Mail Queries: Y   Poetry Collections: N

Helmut Meyer Literary Agency
330 East 79th Street
New York, NY 10021
Phone: (212) 288-2421

Contact: Helmut Meyer
Agency Commission: 15%
Manuscript categories represented:
  General trade nonfiction. Specialize in biography/
  autobiography.
Agency accepts:
  Telephone Queries: Y   Unsolicited Mss: N
  Mail Queries: Y   Poetry Collections: N

Martha Millard Literary Agency
204 Park Avenue
Madison, NJ 07940
Phone: (201) 593-9233 Fax: (201) 593-9235

Contact: Martha Millard
Agency Commission: 15% U.S. print, film, television;
  20% abroad
Manuscript categories represented:
  Book-length fiction and nonfiction. Specialize in cut-
  ting-edge, sophisticated science fiction, horror, fantasy, and mainstream fiction. All popular nonfiction
  and biography, how-to, self-help, and popular
  culture.
Agency accepts:

Telephone Queries: N   Unsolicited Mss: N
Mail Queries: Y   Poetry Collections: N

The Mitnick Agency
91 Henry Street
San Francisco, CA 94114
Phone: (415) 864-2234 Fax: (415) 255-0915

Contact: Samuel A. Mitnick
Agency Commission: 15%
Manuscript categories represented:
   Fiction: mainstream literary, detective, suspense. No science fiction, romance, historical, juvenile, Christian, new age. Short story collections if author has published a novel or placed stories in magazines. Nonfiction: all kinds. No plays or screenplays. Send two sample chapters and synopsis.
Agency accepts:
   Telephone Queries: Y   Unsolicited Mss: N
   Mail Queries: Y   Poetry Collections: N

Moore Literary Agency
4 Dove Street
Newburyport, MA 01950
Phone: (508) 465-9015 Fax: (508) 465-8817

Contact: Claudette Moore
Agency Commission: 15%
Manuscript categories represented:
   Trade computer books.
Agency accepts:

Telephone Queries: N	Unsolicited Mss: Y
Mail Queries: Y	Poetry Collections: N

Howard Morhaim Literary Agency

175 Fifth Avenue
Suite 709
New York, NY 10010
Phone: (212) 529-4433 Fax: (212) 995-1112

Contact: Alison Mullen, Renee Cho
Agency Commission: 15% U.S., 20% abroad
Manuscript categories represented:
  All categories of fiction, nonfiction, and children's
  literature. Specialize in mysteries, thrillers, fantasy,
  science fiction, and children's and young adult books.
Agency accepts:

Telephone Queries: N	Unsolicited Mss: N
Mail Queries: Y	Poetry Collections: N

William Morris Agency

1350 Avenue of the Americas
New York, NY 10019
Phone: (212) 586-5100 Fax: (212) 246-3583

Contact: Literary Department
Agency Commission: 10% U.S., 20% abroad
Manuscript categories represented:
  General fiction and nonfiction. No children's litera-
  ture or poetry.
Agency accepts:

Telephone Queries: N   Unsolicited Mss: N
Mail Queries: Y   Poetry Collections: N

Henry Morrison, Inc.
Box 235
Bedford Hills, NY 10507
Phone: (914) 666-3500 Fax: (914) 241-7846

Contact: Henry Morrison
Agency Commission: 15% U.S., 20% abroad
Manuscript categories represented:
  Novels, some screenplays.
Agency accepts:
  Telephone Queries: N   Unsolicited Mss: N
  Mail Queries: Y   Poetry Collections: N

Jean V. Naggar Literary Agency
216 East 75th Street
New York, NY 10021
Phone: (212) 794-1082

Contact: Jean Naggar, Teresa Cavanaugh
Agency Commission: 15% U.S., 20% abroad
Manuscript categories represented:
  General fiction and general-interest nonfiction.
Agency accepts:
  Telephone Queries: Y   Unsolicited Mss: N
  Mail Queries: Y   Poetry Collections: N

Charles Neighbors

5907 Main Street
Williamsville, NY 14221
Phone: (716) 626-4370/(716) 626-4388

Contact: Charles Neighbors
Agency Commission: 15% books, 20% film and sales
  abroad
Manuscript categories represented:
  General adult trade fiction and nonfiction. Interested
  in just about everything except juvenile trade and
  highly esoteric experimentation.
Agency accepts:
  Telephone Queries: Y   Unsolicited Mss: N
       Mail Queries: Y   Poetry Collections: Y

Regula Noetzli, Literary Agent

444 East 85th Street
New York, NY 10028
Phone: (212) 628-1537 Fax: (212) 744-3145

Contact: Regula Noetzli
Agency Commission: 15%
Manuscript categories represented:
  Adult general fiction and nonfiction. In fiction, spe-
  cialize in mysteries and literary fiction; in nonfiction,
  popular science, psychology, history, and biography.
Agency accepts:
  Telephone Queries: N   Unsolicited Mss: N
       Mail Queries: Y   Poetry Collections: N

The Betsy Nolan Literary Agency
Div. of The Nolan/Lehr Group
50 West 29th Street
Suite 9W
New York, NY 10001
Phone: (212) 779-0700 Fax: (212) 689-0376

Contact: Betsy Nolan
Agency Commission: 15%
Manuscript categories represented:
Fiction and nonfiction. No poetry, children's books, science fiction, or mysteries. Send query letter with no more than 25 to 50 pages of synopsis, plus sample chapters.
Agency accepts:
Telephone Queries: N   Unsolicited Mss: Y
      Mail Queries: Y   Poetry Collections: N

The Norma-Lewis Agency
521 Fifth Avenue, 17th floor
New York, NY 10175
Phone: (212) 751-4955

Contact: Norma Liebert
Agency Commission: 15% U.S. and Canadian, 20% abroad
Manuscript categories represented:
Juvenile fiction and nonfiction, adult fiction, screenplays, stage plays, television scripts.
Agency accepts:
Telephone Queries: N   Unsolicited Mss: N
      Mail Queries: Y   Poetry Collections: N

Harold Ober Associates, Inc.

425 Madison Avenue
New York, NY 10017
Phone: (212) 759-8600 Fax: (212) 759-9428

Contact: Henry Durcow, Claire M. Smith
Agency Commission: 15% U.S., 20% British and trans-
    lation, 10% film
Manuscript categories represented:
    General trade fiction and nonfiction.
Agency accepts:
    Telephone Queries: N   Unsolicited Mss: N
            Mail Queries: Y   Poetry Collections: N

Alice Orr Agency, Inc.

305 Madison Avenue
Suite 1166
New York, NY 10165
Phone: (718) 204-6673 Fax: (718) 204-6023

Contact: Alice Orr
Agency Commission: 15% U.S., 20% abroad
Manuscript categories represented:
    Women's popular fiction, mystery-suspense, com-
    mercial nonfiction.
Agency accepts:
    Telephone Queries: Y   Unsolicited Mss: Y
            Mail Queries: Y   Poetry Collections: N

Fifi Oscard Agency, Inc.
24 West 40th Street, 17th floor
New York, NY 10018
Phone: (212) 764-1100 Fax: (212) 840-5019

Contact: Ivy Fischer Stone
Agency Commission: 15% domestic, 20% abroad
Manuscript categories represented:
Fiction and nonfiction.
Agency accepts:

Telephone Queries: N	Unsolicited Mss: N
Mail Queries: Y	Poetry Collections: N

The Otte Co.
9 Goden Street
Belmont, MA 02178-3002
Phone: (617) 484-8505

Contact: Jane H. Otte
Agency Commission: 15%
Manuscript categories represented:
Adult trade fiction and nonfiction. No poetry, juvenile, young adult, or plays.
Agency accepts:

Telephone Queries: N	Unsolicited Mss: N
Mail Queries: Y	Poetry Collections: N

The Panettieri Agency
142 Marcella Road
Hampton, VA 23666
Phone: (804) 825-1708

Contact: Eugenia Panettieri

Agency Commission: 10% on U.S. sales, 20% on sales abroad

Manuscript categories represented:

Fiction: romance, historical romance, suspense, women's fiction.

Agency accepts:

Telephone Queries: Y	Unsolicited Mss: Y
Mail Queries: Y	Poetry Collections: N

The Richard Parks Agency

138 East 16th Street
Suite 5B
New York, NY 10003
Phone: (212) 254-9067 Fax: (212) 777-4694

Contact: Richard Parks

Agency Commission: 15%

Manuscript categories represented:

General trade fiction and nonfiction for adults (no juvenile).

Agency accepts:

Telephone Queries: N	Unsolicited Mss: N
Mail Queries: Y	Poetry Collections: N

Kathi J. Paton Literary Agency

19 West 55th Street
New York, NY 10019-4907
Phone: (212) 265-6586 Fax: (212) 265-6586

Contact: Kathi Paton

Agency Commission: 15% U.S., 20% with foreign agent

Manuscript categories represented:
   Adult fiction and nonfiction. Specialize in nonfiction:
   business, psychology, biography, sports.
Agency accepts:
   Telephone Queries: Y   Unsolicited Mss: Y
        Mail Queries: Y   Poetry Collections: N

Ray Peekner Literary Agency, Inc.
Box 3308
Bethlehem, PA 18017
Phone: (215) 974-9158 Fax: (215) 974-8228

Contact: Barbara Puechner
Agency Commission: 10% U.S., 20% abroad
Manuscript categories represented:
   Mystery, suspense, women's fiction, Western histor-
   icals. Especially looking for Western historicals and
   mystery/suspense of award-winning quality.
Agency accepts:
   Telephone Queries: Y   Unsolicited Mss: N
        Mail Queries: Y   Poetry Collections: N

L. Perkins
301 West 53rd Street
New York, NY 10019
Phone: (212) 581-7679 Fax: (212) 315-3823

Contact: Lori Perkins
Agency Commission: 15%
Manuscript categories represented:
   In fiction: horror, thrillers, hard-boiled mysteries,
   dark literary fiction. In nonfiction: popular culture.

Agency accepts:
Telephone Queries: N   Unsolicited Mss: N
Mail Queries: Y   Poetry Collections: N

James Peter Associates, Inc.
Box 772
Tenafly, NJ 07670
Phone: (201) 568-0760 Fax: (201) 568-2959

Contact: Bert Holtje
Agency Commission: 15% U.S., 20% abroad
Manuscript categories represented:
Nonfiction books only: all categories, but "we are especially interested in politics, history, popular culture, health, and trade reference projects."
Agency accepts:
Telephone Queries: Y   Unsolicited Mss: N
Mail Queries: Y   Poetry Collections: N

Poirot Literary Agency
2685 Stephens Road
Boulder, CO 80303
Phone: (303) 494-6382 Fax: (303) 494-9396

Contact: Henry Poirot
Agency Commission: 10% U.S., 20% abroad
Manuscript categories represented:
Nonfiction; some mysteries. No computer books.
Agency accepts:
Telephone Queries: Y   Unsolicited Mss: N
Mail Queries: Y   Poetry Collections: N

Susan Ann Protter, Literary Agent
110 West 40th Street
Suite 1408
New York, NY 10018
Phone: (212) 840-0480

Contact: Susan Ann Protter
Agency Commission: 15%
Manuscript categories represented:
  Nonfiction and fiction, including thrillers, mysteries, science fiction, and fantasy. Especially seeking quality nonfiction and literate fiction. Short story collections only if author has published. Keep queries brief and please indicate where you discovered agency's listing.
Agency accepts:
  Telephone Queries: N   Unsolicited Mss: N
      Mail Queries: Y   Poetry Collections: N

Roberta Pryor, Inc.
24 West 55th Street
New York, NY 10019
Phone: (212) 245-0420 Fax: (212) 757-8030

Contact: David Kidd
Agency Commission: 10%
Manuscript categories represented:
  Fiction and nonfiction of all types, but no science fiction or new age books. "Poetry collections very rarely: accomplished poets who stand a chance at being published usually have better contacts than we do."

Agency accepts:
Telephone Queries: N   Unsolicited Mss: N
Mail Queries: Y   Poetry Collections: N

Quicksilver Books, Inc.
Literary Agents
50 Wilson Street
Hartsdale, NY 10530
Phone: (914) 946-8748

Contact: Bob Silverstein, Pres.
Agency Commission: 15% U.S. (print, film); 20%
abroad
Manuscript categories represented:
Literary and commercial fiction and nonfiction. Quality fiction—mainstream markets only. In nonfiction: psychology, self-help, new age, holistic health, environment/ecology.
Agency accepts:
Telephone Queries: Y   Unsolicited Mss: N
Mail Queries: Y   Poetry Collections: N

Charlotte Cecil Raymond, Literary Agent
32 Bradlee Road
Marblehead, MA 01945
Phone: (617) 631-6722

Contact: Charlotte Cecil Raymond
Agency Commission: 15%
Manuscript categories represented:
Nonfiction, fiction; no poetry, screenplays, or short

stories. Unsolicited queries and manuscripts should include proposal and sample chapters.

Agency accepts:

Telephone Queries: Y   Unsolicited Mss: Y

Mail Queries: Y   Poetry Collections: N

Helen Rees Literary Agency

308 Commonwealth Avenue

Boston, MA 02116

Phone: (617) 262-2401 Fax: (617) 262-2401

Contact: Helen Rees

Agency Commission: 15%

Manuscript categories represented:

Fiction and nonfiction

Agency accepts:

Telephone Queries: N   Unsolicited Mss: Y

Mail Queries: Y   Poetry Collections: N

Rhodes Literary Agency

140 West End Avenue

New York, NY 10023

Phone: (212) 580-1300

Contact: Joseph Rhodes

Agency Commission: 15%

Manuscript categories represented:

Fiction and nonfiction, adult and juvenile.

Agency accepts:

Telephone Queries: N   Unsolicited Mss: N

Mail Queries: Y   Poetry Collections: N

The Robbins Office, Inc.
2 Dag Hammarskjold Plaza
866 Second Avenue, 12th floor
New York, NY 10017
Phone: (212) 223-0720 Fax: (212) 223-2535

Contact: Julia Null
Agency Commission: 15%
Manuscript categories represented:
   General fiction, narrative nonfiction, memoir, auto-
   biography, biography, investigative reporting. No un-
   solicited proposals or manuscripts; by referral only.
Agency accepts:
   Telephone Queries: N   Unsolicited Mss: N
   Mail Queries: N   Poetry Collections: N

Rosenstone/Wender
3 East 48th Street, 4th floor
New York, NY 10017
Phone: (212) 832-8330 Fax: (212) 759-4524

Contact: Phyllis Wender, Susan Perlman
Agency Commission: 15% U.S., 20% abroad
Manuscript categories represented:
   Fiction and nonfiction.
Agency accepts:
   Telephone Queries: N   Unsolicited Mss: N
   Mail Queries: Y   Poetry Collections: N

Jane Rotrosen Agency
318 East 51st Street
New York, NY 10022
Phone: (212) 593-4330 Fax: (212) 935-6985

Contact: Stephanie Laidman
Agency Commission: 15% U.S. and Canada
Manuscript categories represented:
All fiction and nonfiction: commercial fiction, including romance and science fiction; children's literature; cookbooks.
Agency accepts:
Telephone Queries: N   Unsolicited Mss: N
     Mail Queries: Y   Poetry Collections: N

Russell & Volkening, Inc.
50 West 29th Street
New York, NY 10001
Phone: (212) 684-6050 Fax: (212) 889-3026

Contact: Timothy Seldes, Miriam Altshuler
Agency Commission: 10% U.S., "higher" for sales abroad
Manuscript categories represented:
Literary fiction and nonfiction. No poetry, "with regret."
Agency accepts:
Telephone Queries: N   Unsolicited Mss: N
     Mail Queries: Y   Poetry Collections: N

The Sagalyn Literary Agency
4825 Bethesda Avenue, Suite 302
Bethesda, MD 20814
Phone: (301) 718-6440

Contact: Raphael Sagalyn
Agency Commission: not specified
Manuscript categories represented:

Adult fiction and nonfiction. "The query letter is a crucial and often overlooked part of the publishing process."

Agency accepts:

Telephone Queries: Y   Unsolicited Mss: N
Mail Queries: Y   Poetry Collections: N

Sandum & Associates

144 East 84th Street
New York, NY 10028
Phone: (212) 737-2011

Contact: Howard E. Sandum
Agency Commission: 15% on U.S. book sales
Manuscript categories represented:
All categories of adult books: general nonfiction, commercial and literary fiction. No children's books.
Unsolicited manuscripts are "rarely" considered.

Agency accepts:

Telephone Queries: N   Unsolicited Mss: Y
Mail Queries: Y   Poetry Collections: N

Schaffner Agency, Inc.

6625 Casas Adobes Road
Tucson, AZ 85704
Phone: (602) 797-8000 Fax: (602) 797-8271

Contact: Timothy Schaffner, Jennifer Powers
Agency Commission: Standard
Manuscript categories represented:
Specialize in environmental nonfiction; also interested in quality adult fiction and biographies.

Agency accepts:
Telephone Queries: Y · Unsolicited Mss: N
Mail Queries: Y · Poetry Collections: Y

Schlessinger–Van Dyck Agency

Literary & Publicity Services
2814 PSFS Bldg, 12 S. 12th St.
Philadelphia, PA 19107
Phone: (215) 627-4665 Fax: (215) 627-0488

Contact: Barrie Van Dyck, Blanche Schlessinger
Agency Commission: 15%
Manuscript categories represented:
General nonfiction; literary and commercial fiction; children's books. Specialize in biography, cookbooks, how-to, medical, general reference, mysteries, children's books.
Agency accepts:
Telephone Queries: N · Unsolicited Mss: Y
Mail Queries: Y · Poetry Collections: N

Susan Schulman Literary Agency

454 West 44th Street
New York, NY 10036
Phone: (212) 713-1633 Fax: (212) 581-8830

Contact: Susan Schulman
Agency Commission: 10% U.S., 20% abroad
Manuscript categories represented:
Fiction and nonfiction. Specialize in women's issues and contemporary women's fiction, mystery, and science/social science.

Agency accepts:
Telephone Queries: N   Unsolicited Mss: N
Mail Queries: Y   Poetry Collections: N

"$50 to evaluate a manuscript of any length if submittor insists on an evaluation. Not a business we prefer to do, so we are willing to offer the service, but not to finance it."

Laurens R. Schwartz, Esq.
Literary Representative
5 East 22nd Street
Suite 15D
New York, NY 10010-5315
Phone: (212) 228-2614 Fax: (212) 228-2614

Contact: Laurens R. Schwartz
Agency Commission: Varies, but generally 12.5% U.S., 20% abroad
Manuscript categories represented:
All areas except poetry.
Agency accepts:
Telephone Queries: N   Unsolicited Mss: N
Mail Queries: Y   Poetry Collections: N

Charlotte Sheedy Literary Agency, Inc.
41 King Street
New York, NY 10014
Phone: (212) 633-2288 Fax: (212) 633-6261

Contact: Charlotte Sheedy
Agency Commission: 15%

Manuscript categories represented:
Fiction and nonfiction; no children's books.
Agency accepts:

Telephone Queries: Y	Unsolicited Mss: Y
Mail Queries: Y	Poetry Collections: N

The Shepard Agency
73 Kingswood Drive
Bethel, CT 06801
Phone: (203) 790-4230 Fax: (203) 743-1879

Contact: Jean Shepard
Agency Commission: 15%
Manuscript categories represented:
Adult fiction and nonfiction—very little in young adult or children's categories. Specialize in nonfiction: business, self-help, inspirational, nutrition and food. No pornography.
Agency accepts:

Telephone Queries: Y	Unsolicited Mss: N
Mail Queries: Y	Poetry Collections: N

Bobbe Siegel, Rights & Literary Agent
41 West 83rd Street
New York, NY 10024
Phone: (212) 877-4985 Fax: (212) 877-4985

Contact: Bobbe Siegel
Agency Commission: 15%
Manuscript categories represented:
Fiction: women's, mystery, suspense, literary, his-

torical, fantasy. Nonfiction: biography, how-to, psychology, true crime.
Agency accepts:

Telephone Queries: N	Unsolicited Mss: N
Mail Queries: Y	Poetry Collections: N

Jacqueline Simenauer Literary Agency, Inc.
14 Capron Lane
Upper Montclair, NJ 07043
Phone: (201) 746-0539 Fax: (201) 746-0754

Contact: Jacqueline Simenauer, Robin Pearson
Agency Commission: 10%–15% U.S., 20% abroad
Manuscript categories represented:
  Nonfiction; some novels. Specialize in psychiatry and psychology; represent psychiatrists, psychologists, and other mental-health professionals exclusively.
Agency accepts:

Telephone Queries: Y	Unsolicited Mss: N
Mail Queries: Y	Poetry Collections: N

Valerie Smith, Literary Agent
R.D. Box 160, Rte 44–55
Modena, NY 12548
Phone: (914) 883-5848

Contact: Valerie Smith
Agency Commission: 15% U.S.
Manuscript categories represented:
  Fiction, especially fantasy and science fiction.
Agency accepts:

Telephone Queries: N   Unsolicited Mss: N
Mail Queries: Y   Poetry Collections: N

Sobel Weber Associates, Inc.
146 East 19th Street
New York, NY 10003
Phone: (212) 420-8585 Fax: (212) 505-1017

Contact: Nat Sobel
Agency Commission: 15%
Manuscript categories represented:
Serious fiction, mysteries, cookbooks, serious nonfiction.
Agency accepts:
Telephone Queries: N   Unsolicited Mss: N
Mail Queries: Y   Poetry Collections: N

Elyse Sommer, Inc.
110–34 73rd Road
P.O. Box 1133
Forest Hills, NY 11375
Phone: (718) 263-2668

Contact: Elyse Sommer
Agency Commission: 10% if over $25K; 15% if under;
20% abroad
Manuscript categories represented:
Nonfiction. Specialize in popular, one-volume reference books (e.g., workbooks, dictionaries, history books).
Agency accepts:

Telephone Queries: Y   Unsolicited Mss: Y
Mail Queries: Y   Poetry Collections: N

Prefers mail queries with great detail.

Philip G. Spitzer Literary Agency
788 Ninth Avenue
New York, NY 10019
Phone: (212) 265-6003 Fax: (212) 765-0953

Contact: Philip Spitzer
Agency Commission: 15%
Manuscript categories represented:
  General fiction and nonfiction. Especially interested
  in literary fiction and thrillers; in nonfiction, politics,
  biography, social issues, sports.
Agency accepts:
  Telephone Queries: N   Unsolicited Mss: N
  Mail Queries: Y   Poetry Collections: N

Lyle Steele & Co., Ltd., Literary Agents
511 East 73rd Street
Suite 7
New York, NY 10021
Phone: (212) 288-2981 Fax: (212) 288-2981

Contact: Lyle Steele
Agency Commission: 10%
Manuscript categories represented:
  Mystery, horror, suspense, historical, children's,
  non-illustrated nonfiction, gay and lesbian. Specialize

in health, self-help, parenting, current events, and controversial subjects.

Agency accepts:

Telephone Queries: N	Unsolicited Mss: Y
Mail Queries: Y	Poetry Collections: N

Stepping Stone Literary Agency, Inc.

59 West 71st Street
New York, NY 10023
Phone: (212) 362-9277 Fax: (212) 362-1998

Contact: Sarah Jane Freymann
Agency Commission: 15%
Manuscript categories represented:
  Mainstream and literary fiction. Hardcover mystery and suspense; general nonfiction—coffee table books, lifestyle.
Agency accepts:

Telephone Queries: Y	Unsolicited Mss: N
Mail Queries: Y	Poetry Collections: N

Sterling Lord Literistic, Inc.

One Madison Avenue
New York, NY 10010
Phone: (212) 696-2800 Fax: (212) 686-6976

Contact: not specified
Agency Commission: 10% U.S. and abroad
Manuscript categories represented:
  General fiction and nonfiction; juvenile; poetry.
Agency accepts:

Telephone Queries: N   Unsolicited Mss: Y
Mail Queries: Y   Poetry Collections: Y

Gloria Stern Agency
1230 Park Avenue
New York, NY 10128
Phone: (212) 289-7698

Contact: Gloria Stern
Agency Commission: 15%
Manuscript categories represented:
History, biography, education, health, women's issues, serious fiction.
Agency accepts:
Telephone Queries: Y   Unsolicited Mss: N
Mail Queries: Y   Poetry Collections: N

Jo Stewart Agency
201 East 66th Street
Suite 18G
New York, NY 10021
Phone: (212) 879-1301

Contact: Jo Stewart
Agency Commission: not specified
Manuscript categories represented:
Fiction and nonfiction. No science fiction or fantasy.
Prefer mail query before unsolicited manuscript.
Agency accepts:
Telephone Queries: N   Unsolicited Mss: Y
Mail Queries: Y   Poetry Collections: N

Robin Straus Agency, Inc.
229 East 79th Street
New York, NY 10021
Phone: (212) 472-3282 Fax: (212) 472-3833

Contact: Robin Straus
Agency Commission: not specified
Manuscript categories represented:
  Adult fiction and nonfiction; juvenile.
Agency accepts:
  Telephone Queries: Y   Unsolicited Mss: Y
        Mail Queries: Y   Poetry Collections: N

Gunther Stuhlmann, Author's Representative
P.O. Box 276
Becket, MA 01223
Phone: (413) 623-5170

Contact: Barbara Ward
Agency Commission: 10% U.S., 15% Britain &
  Commonwealth
Manuscript categories represented:
  Book-length material only. High-quality literary fiction, biography, nonfiction. No short stories, poetry, plays, detective fiction, unsolicited screenplays (television or film).
Agency accepts:
  Telephone Queries: N   Unsolicited Mss: N
        Mail Queries: Y   Poetry Collections: N

H.N. Swanson, Inc.
8523 Sunset Boulevard
Los Angeles, CA 90069
Phone: (213) 652-5385 Fax: (213) 652-3690

Contact: Thomas Shanks
Agency Commission: 10%
Manuscript categories represented:
  Most categories. Specialize in fiction.
Agency accepts:

Telephone Queries: N	Unsolicited Mss: N
Mail Queries: Y	Poetry Collections: N

TARC Literary Agency
P.O. Box 64785
Tucson, AZ 85740-1785
Phone: (602) 325-4733

Contact: Martha R. Gore
Agency Commission: 15% U.S., 20% abroad
Manuscript categories represented:
  Book-length material only. Fiction: mainstream, modern Western, crime, mystery; no romance, science fiction, horror, fantasy. Nonfiction: self-help written by professionals for the commercial bookstore trade.
Agency accepts:

Telephone Queries: N	Unsolicited Mss: N
Mail Queries: Y	Poetry Collections: N

"We also supply ghostwriters and coauthors for a fee for manuscripts we intend to agent."

Roslyn Targ Literary Agency
105 West 13th Street
Suite 15E
New York, NY 10011
Phone: (212) 206-9390 Fax: (212) 989-6233

Contact: Roslyn Targ
Agency Commission: 15% unpublished writers, 10% published
Manuscript categories represented:
Nonfiction and fiction. No poetry or humor books. Unsolicited manuscripts considered "only if I receive a query first."
Agency accepts:

Telephone Queries: N	Unsolicited Mss: Y
Mail Queries: Y	Poetry Collections: N

Dawson Taylor
4722 Holly Lake Drive
Lake Worth, FL 33463
Phone: (407) 965-4150

Contact: Dawson Taylor
Agency Commission: 15%
Manuscript categories represented:
All nonfiction: specialize in sports (especially golf and bowling), true crime, medical, psychological.
Agency accepts:

Telephone Queries: N	Unsolicited Mss: N
Mail Queries: Y	Poetry Collections: N

2M Communications, Ltd.
121 West 27th Street
New York, NY 10001
Phone: (212) 741-1509 Fax: (212) 691-4460

Contact: Madeleine Morel
Agency Commission: 15%
Manuscript categories represented:
  Nonfiction: cookbooks, popular psychology, health, medical, biography, popular culture, business.
Agency accepts:

Telephone Queries: Y	Unsolicited Mss: N
Mail Queries: Y	Poetry Collections: N

Susan P. Urstadt, Inc.
Box 1676
New Canaan, CT 06840
Phone: (203) 966-6111 Fax: (203) 966-2249

Contact: Susan P. Urstadt
Agency Commission: 15% U.S., 20% abroad
Manuscript categories represented:
  Quality nonfiction: popular reference, current affairs, gardening, antiques and decorative arts, illustrated books, travel, food, cooking and wine, crafts, collectibles, history, sports, biography, performing arts. "No unsolicited fiction please."
Agency accepts:

Telephone Queries: N	Unsolicited Mss: N
Mail Queries: Y	Poetry Collections: N

Van der Leun & Associates
464 Mill Hill Drive
Southport, CT 06490
Phone: (203) 259-4897

Contact: Patricia Van der Leun
Agency Commission: 15%
Manuscript categories represented:
  Nonfiction: popular science, art and architecture, biography. Translations. Literary and commercial fiction.
Agency accepts:
  Telephone Queries: N   Unsolicited Mss: N
         Mail Queries: Y   Poetry Collections: N

Wallace Literary Agency, Inc.
177 East 70th Street
New York, NY 10021
Phone: (212) 570-9090 Fax: (212) 772-8979

Contact: Lois Wallace, Thomas C. Wallace
Agency Commission: 10% books, 15% magazines, 20% sales abroad
Manuscript categories represented:
  Literary fiction, literary biographies, serious nonfiction.
Agency accepts:
  Telephone Queries: N   Unsolicited Mss: N
         Mail Queries: Y   Poetry Collections: N

John A. Ware Literary Agency
392 Central Park West
New York, NY 10025
Phone: (212) 866-4733

Contact: John A. Ware
Agency Commission: 10% U.S., 20% for foreign rights
sales
Manuscript categories represented:
Biography, history, current affairs, investigative journalism, science, health and medicine (proper credentials required), "inside look" books, sports, folklore, Americana; thrillers, mysteries, and literary but accessible fiction, non-category.
Agency accepts:

Telephone Queries: N	Unsolicited Mss: N
Mail Queries: Y	Poetry Collections: N

Harriet Wasserman Literary Agency, Inc.
137 East 36th Street
New York, NY 10016
Phone: (212) 689-3257

Contact: Harriet Wasserman
Agency Commission: 10% U.S., film, first serial; 20%
abroad
Manuscript categories represented:
Quality fiction and nonfiction.
Agency accepts:

Telephone Queries: N	Unsolicited Mss: N
Mail Queries: N	Poetry Collections: N

Watkins Loomis Agency, Inc.
133 East 35th Street
Suite 1
New York, NY 10016
Phone: (212) 532-0080 Fax: (212) 889-0506

Contact: Gloria Loomis
Agency Commission: 10%
Manuscript categories represented:
  Specialize in literary fiction, literary biography, political journalism, nonfiction on the arts.
Agency accepts:
  Telephone Queries: N   Unsolicited Mss: N
         Mail Queries: Y   Poetry Collections: N

Sandra Watt & Associates
8033 Sunset Boulevard
Suite 4053
Los Angeles, CA 90046
Phone: (213) 653-2339

Contact: David Smith
Agency Commission: 10% screenplays, 15% books
Manuscript categories represented:
  Nonfiction: animals, anthropology, archaeology, popular science, reference, true crime, self-help, cookbooks. Fiction: detective/police, crime, mystery, suspense, thriller, glitz, women's fiction. Specialize in true crime, suspense, self-help, popular science, and reference.

Agency accepts:
Telephone Queries: N   Unsolicited Mss: N
Mail Queries: Y   Poetry Collections: N

Marketing fee of $100 is charged to previously unpublished authors, after agency contract is signed, to defray postage and telephone expenses.

The Wendy Weil Agency, Inc.
747 Third Avenue
New York, NY 10017
Phone: (212) 753-2605 Fax: (212) 688-8297

Contact: Wendy Weil
Agency Commission: 10% U.S., 20% abroad
Manuscript categories represented:
Fiction and nonfiction. No screenplays, children's literature, or poetry.
Agency accepts:
Telephone Queries: N   Unsolicited Mss: N
Mail Queries: Y   Poetry Collections: N

Cherry Weiner Literary Agency
28 Kipling Way
Manalapan, NJ 07726
Phone: (908) 446-2096

Contact: Cherry Weiner
Agency Commission: 15%
Manuscript categories represented:
Fiction: science fiction, fantasy, romance, mystery, mainstream, Western. "Only recommended writers

are considered—or those personally met at conferences."

Agency accepts:

Telephone Queries: N   Unsolicited Mss: N
          Mail Queries: N   Poetry Collections: N

Wieser & Wieser, Inc.
118 East 25th Street
2nd Floor
New York, NY 10010
Phone: (212) 260-0860 Fax: (212) 505-7186

Contact: Olga B. Wieser
Agency Commission: 15% U.S., 20% abroad, 15% dramatic
Manuscript categories represented:
Mainstream fiction, literary fiction; general nonfiction—environmental, communications, finance.

Agency accepts:

Telephone Queries: Y   Unsolicited Mss: N
          Mail Queries: Y   Poetry Collections: N

Rhoda Weyr Agency
151 Bergen Street
Brooklyn, NY 11217
Phone: (718) 522-0480 Fax: (718) 522-0410

Contact: Rhoda Weyr
Agency Commission: 15% U.S., 20% abroad
Manuscript categories represented:
General fiction and nonfiction. Considers unsolicited manuscripts on an exclusive basis only.

Agency accepts:
Telephone Queries: N   Unsolicited Mss: Y
Mail Queries: Y   Poetry Collections: N

Witherspoon & Chernoff Associates, Inc.
130 West 57th Street
Suite 14C
New York, NY 10019
Phone: (212) 757-0567 Fax: (212) 757-2982

Contact: Kimberly Witherspoon, Dona Chernoff
Agency Commission: 15% U.S., 20% abroad
Manuscript categories represented:
All categories of fiction and nonfiction. Poetry collections considered when preceded by a query.
Agency accepts:
Telephone Queries: N   Unsolicited Mss: N
Mail Queries: Y   Poetry Collections: Y

Ruth Wreschner, Authors' Representative
10 West 74th Street
New York, NY 10023
Phone: (212) 877-2605 Fax: (212) 595-5843

Contact: Ruth Wreschner
Agency Commission: 15% U.S., 20% abroad
Manuscript categories represented:
Nonfiction, especially popular medicine and psychology. Fiction: mainstream; genre books, particularly mysteries.
Agency accepts:

Telephone Queries: Y   Unsolicited Mss: N
Mail Queries: Y   Poetry Collections: N

Writers House, Inc.
21 West 26th Street
New York, NY 10010
Phone: (212) 685-2400 Fax: (212) 685-1781

Contact: Sheila Callahan
Agency Commission: 10% juvenile, 15% adult, 20% sales abroad
Manuscript categories represented:
All trade categories except poetry, original film, television and stage scripts, short stories, and magazine articles. Especially interested in suspense novels and juvenile and young adult series.
Agency accepts:
Telephone Queries: N   Unsolicited Mss: Y
Mail Queries: Y   Poetry Collections: N

Writers' Productions
P.O. Box 630
Westport, CT 06881
Phone: (203) 227-8199 Fax: (203) 227-6349
Contact: David L. Meth
Agency Commission: 15% U.S., 20%–25% dramatic and sales abroad
Manuscript categories represented:
Quality literary fiction and nonfiction with special interest in works about Asia, especially Japan. "We do not evaluate manuscripts."

Agency accepts:
    Telephone Queries: N   Unsolicited Mss: Y
        Mail Queries: Y   Poetry Collections: N

Mary Yost Associates, Inc.
59 East 54th Street
New York, NY 10022
Phone: (212) 980-4988 Fax: (212) 935-3632

Contact: Mary Yost
Agency Commission: 15%
Manuscript categories represented:
  Psychology, biography, women's studies, fiction,
  medical new age.
Agency accepts:
    Telephone Queries: N   Unsolicited Mss: Y
        Mail Queries: Y   Poetry Collections: N

Susan Zeckendorf Associates, Inc.
171 West 57th Street, #11B
New York, NY 10019
Phone: (212) 245-2928

Contact: Susan Zeckendorf
Agency Commission: 15%
Manuscript categories represented:
  Literary fiction, women's commercial fiction, mys-
  teries, thrillers; parenting, music, science—"every-
  thing except science fiction and romances."
Agency accepts:

Telephone Queries: N   Unsolicited Mss: N
Mail Queries: Y   Poetry Collections: N

George Ziegler
160 East 97th Street
Suite 4A
New York, NY 10029
Phone: (212) 348-3637 Fax: (212) 546-1958

Contact: George Ziegler
Agency Commission: 15%
Manuscript categories represented:
Book-length nonfiction. "Re: mail queries—if you
have to put more than 29 cents postage on it, you're
sending too much. If you don't enclose an SASE, you
won't get an answer unless your letter is irresistible."
Agency accepts:
Telephone Queries: N   Unsolicited Mss: N
Mail Queries: Y   Poetry Collections: N

FEE-CHARGING
AGENCIES:
AN ANNOTATED LIST

The thirty-seven agencies listed here consider unsolicited (unreferred) material for a fee. Most of them explain their fee structure and what the writer receives; in some cases, the fee is refundable in the event of a sale.

For a discussion of fee-charging agents, see Chapter Six of this book. It is not necessary to pay a fee in order to find a literary agent, and the evaluation of a manuscript as part of a workshop may be a better buy than what a fee-charging agent offers. The information listed here is presented in order to help the buyer—the writer—make an informed decision.

Again, a self-addressed, stamped envelope should always be included with any correspondence to any agent.

This list was compiled from questionnaires Poets &

Writers, Inc., sent to all 472 literary agencies listed in the 1991 *Literary Market Place* (R.R. Bowker Company, 1991); 240 agencies—51 percent—responded.

Authors Marketing Services, Ltd.

217 Degrassi Street
Toronto, Ontario M4M 2KB
Canada
Phone: (416) 463-7200 Fax: (416) 469-4494

Contact: Larry Hoffman
Agency Commission: 15% for Canada and the U.S.,
  20% elsewhere
Manuscript categories represented:
  Fiction and nonfiction (self-help, parenting, business, biography). Specialize in fiction and in self-help.
Agency accepts:

Telephone Queries: Y	Unsolicited Mss: N
Mail Queries: Y	Poetry Collections: N

"We charge a fee only to unpublished novelists, as we read only entire novels. All else is proposal form, and hence, no fee."

Elizabeth H. Backman

Box 536
Johnnycake Hollow Road
Pine Plains, NY 12567
Phone: (518) 398-6408 Fax: (518) 398-6449

Contact: Elizabeth H. Backman

Agency Commission: 15% plus expenses (postage, phone, copying)

Manuscript categories represented:

Nonfiction: biography, politics, current events, true crime, business, memoirs, social history, self-help, science, sports, cooking, humor, arts/crafts, health, popular culture, popular reference. Fiction: mysteries, historicals, regionals, women's contemporary fiction, men's adventure.

Agency accepts:

Telephone Queries: Y   Unsolicited Mss: N
        Mail Queries: Y   Poetry Collections: N

"I charge a $50 reading fee for completed manuscripts and $25 for book proposals with three sample chapters."

Meredith G. Bernstein
2112 Broadway
Suite 503A
New York, NY 10023
Phone: (212) 799-1007 Fax: (212) 799-1145

Contact: Meredith Bernstein, Elizabeth Cavanaugh
Agency Commission: 15% U.S., 20% abroad
Manuscript categories represented:

All but young adult, juvenile, and Westerns. Specialize in nonfiction and commercial and genre fiction.

Agency accepts:

Telephone Queries: Y   Unsolicited Mss: N
Mail Queries: Y   Poetry Collections: N

If author is unpublished in book form, $50 for outline and three sample chapters.

Pema Browne, Ltd.
Box 104B
Pine Road
Neversink, NY 12765
Phone: (914) 985-2936 Fax: (914) 985-7635

Contact: Pema Browne or Perry Browne
Agency Commission: 15%
Manuscript categories represented:
  Fiction and nonfiction, adult and juvenile; all mass market categories. "Any category as long as the manuscript is viable."
Agency accepts:
  Telephone Queries: N   Unsolicited Mss: N
  Mail Queries: Y   Poetry Collections: N

Fee depends upon word count.

Dorese Agency, Ltd.
37965 Palo Verde Drive
Cathedral City, CA 92234
Phone: (619) 321-1115 Fax: (619) 321-1049

Contact: Alyss Dorese
Agency Commission: 15%

Manuscript categories represented:
Fiction, nonfiction. Specialize in true crime, nonfiction.
Agency accepts:

Telephone Queries: Y	Unsolicited Mss: N
Mail Queries: Y	Poetry Collections: N

Fee charged if author is not referred by a professional or has not been published.

Robert L. Fenton PC Law Offices
31800 Northwestern Hwy.
Suite 390
Farmington Hills, MI 48334
Phone: (313) 855-8780 Fax: (313) 855-3302

Contact: Robert L. Fenton
Agency Commission: 15% U.S.
Manuscript categories represented:
Fiction (50%), nonfiction (20%), movie scripts (15%), television scripts (15%). 75% of business is derived from commissions on manuscript sales; 25% from reading fees or criticism service. Payment of a criticism fee does not ensure representation.
Agency accepts:

Telephone Queries: Y	Unsolicited Mss: N
Mail Queries: Y	Poetry Collections: N

"To waive reading fee, author must have been published at least three times by a mainline New York publishing house." Criticism service: $350.

Frieda Fishbein, Ltd.
2556 Hubbard Street
Brooklyn, NY 11235
Phone: (212) 247-4398

Contact: Janice Fishbein
Agency Commission: 10% U.S., 15% abroad
Manuscript categories represented:
  All categories except short stories, books for young children, and poetry.
Agency accepts:

Telephone Queries: N	Unsolicited Mss: N
Mail Queries: Y	Poetry Collections: N

$75 for first 50,000 words; $1 per thousand words thereafter. Fee charged 75% of the time, depending on writer's background.

Peter Fleming Agency
Box 458
Pacific Palisades, CA 90272
Phone: (213) 271-5693 Fax: (213) 454-4491

Contact: Peter Fleming, Neil Burkhardt
Agency Commission: 15%
Manuscript categories represented:
  Nonfiction and fiction with best-selling potential. "I'll consider anything that looks successful! I prefer innovative, helpful books written by people with credible expertise in their field (regardless of their field)."
Agency accepts:

Telephone Queries: Y	Unsolicited Mss: N
Mail Queries: Y	Poetry Collections: N

"Although I have not charged a fee for reading in more than four years, I do reserve the right to do so if appropriate."

Gelles-Cole Literary Enterprises

320 East 42nd Street
Suite 411
New York, NY 10017
Phone: (212) 573-9857

Contact: Sandi Gelles-Cole
Agency Commission: 15% U.S., 20% abroad
Manuscript categories represented:
    Fiction and nonfiction. Specialize in popular (as opposed to literary) fiction, nonfiction that is women-oriented, popular psychology. No category fiction.
Agency accepts:

Telephone Queries: N	Unsolicited Mss: N
Mail Queries: Y	Poetry Collections: N

Reading fees: $50 for proposal, $79 for manuscript under 80,000 words, $95 for manuscripts over 80,000 words.

Carolyn Jenks Agency

205 Walden Street
Cambridge, MA 02140
Phone: (617) 876-6927 Fax: (617) 876-6927

Contact: Carolyn Jenks
Agency Commission: 15%
Manuscript categories represented:
Fiction, nonfiction, screenplays, television scripts. "I specialize in identifying, nurturing, and marketing unknown, potentially highly commercial writers. I participate in all major decisions (and minor) along the way leading to the author's establishment in competitive markets."
Agency accepts:

Telephone Queries: N	Unsolicited Mss: N
Mail Queries: Y	Poetry Collections: N

Fiction or nonfiction: $60, under 500 pages; $100, over 500 pages. $200 for editing and development. Clients under contract to the agency are not charged the above fees.

Larry Kaltman
1301 South Scott Street
Arlington, VA 22204
Phone: (703) 920-3771

Contact: Larry Kaltman
Agency Commission: 15%
Manuscript categories represented:
Fiction, all categories. In nonfiction, specialize in health/medicine, science/technology, self-help, and sports. Sponsors the Washington Prize for Fiction.
Agency accepts:

Telephone Queries: Y   Unsolicited Mss: N
Mail Queries: Y   Poetry Collections: N

Manuscripts up to 300 pages, $150; each additional page, $0.50. Author receives a report (approximately 1,500 words) on literary quality, structure and organization, and estimate of marketability. Report furnished in about two weeks.

Kellock & Associates, Ltd.
11017 80th Avenue
Edmonton, AB T6G 0R2
Canada
Phone: (403) 433-0274 Fax: (403) 439-9649

Contact: Joanne Kellock
Agency Commission: 15% English language; 20% abroad
Manuscript categories represented:
Fiction: commercial, genre, literary. Nonfiction: biography, history, how-to, upmarket new age, business, travel/adventure—everything except current Christian born-again, downmarket new age. All works for children from the picture book to the young adult in both fiction and nonfiction.
Agency accepts:
Telephone Queries: Y   Unsolicited Mss: N
Mail Queries: Y   Poetry Collections: N

Fees charged to unpublished writers. $50 for complete children's picture book; $75 for three chapters plus brief synopsis of any adult work, fiction or nonfiction. If work is promising, balance read for free.

Lighthouse Literary Agency
P.O. Box 1000
Edgewater, FL 32132-1000
Phone: (904) 345-1515 Fax: (904) 345-1515

Contact: Sandra Kangas
Agency Commission: 15% U.S., 20% abroad, 10%–15% screenplays
Manuscript categories represented:
  Poetry in book-length collections, screenplays, juvenile and adult book-length fiction and nonfiction.
Agency accepts:

Telephone Queries: Y	Unsolicited Mss: Y
Mail Queries: Y	Poetry Collections: Y

No charge for brief proposals, queries, our clients, client or publisher referrals, and currently published/produced writers. "We enjoy working with new writers, from whom we have discovered some of our best works. For such new writers, $45 should accompany the submission."

Denise Marcil Literary Agency, Inc.
685 West End Avenue, Apt 9C
New York, NY 10025
Phone: (212) 932-3110 Fax: (212) 932-3113

Contact: Denise Marcil
Agency Commission: not specified

Manuscript categories represented:
   Commercial fiction and nonfiction, especially women's fiction, romance, business, finance, careers, self-help, parenting, women's issues.
Agency accepts:
   Telephone Queries: Y   Unsolicited Mss: N
          Mail Queries: Y   Poetry Collections: N

"Based on a query, I may request three chapters and outline (fiction) or a proposal and chapter (nonfiction). Only if I request the material do I charge a $45 fee. If I like the sample material, I'll request the remainder of the manuscript with no additional fees."

Betty Marks
176 East 77th Street, Apt 9F
New York, NY 10021
Phone: (212) 535-8388

Contact: Betty Marks
Agency Commission: 15%
Manuscript categories represented:
   Fiction and nonfiction.
Agency accepts:
   Telephone Queries: Y   Unsolicited Mss: N
          Mail Queries: Y   Poetry Collections: N

For previously unpublished writers, fee of $250 for a manuscript up to 100,000 words. Criticism given in letter form within 2 to 3 weeks.

Scott Meredith Literary Agency, Inc.
845 Third Avenue
New York, NY 10022
Phone: (212) 245-5500 Fax: (212) 755-2972

Contact: Scott Meredith
Agency Commission: 10% U.S., 20% abroad
Manuscript categories represented:
General fiction and nonfiction, adult and juvenile; books, articles, short stories, plays.
Agency accepts:

Telephone Queries: Y	Unsolicited Mss: Y
Mail Queries: Y	Poetry Collections: Y

Fees charged to unpublished authors.

The Peter Miller Agency, Inc.
Subs. of Lion Entertainment
Box 790, Old Chelsea Station
New York, NY 10011
Phone: (212) 929-1222 Fax: (212) 206-0238

Contact: Peter Miller
Agency Commission: 10%–15%
Manuscript categories represented:
Nonfiction, including biographies, cookbooks, self-help, and how-to. Fiction of all kinds. Specialize in true crime, Hollywood history, and all books with motion picture and television production potential.
Agency accepts:

Telephone Queries: N	Unsolicited Mss: Y
Mail Queries: Y	Poetry Collections: N

Fees charged for unsolicited manuscripts (not for queries or proposals).

B.K. Nelson Literary Agency
84 Woodland Road
Pleasantville, NY 10570
Phone: (914) 741-1322 Fax: (914) 741-1324

Contact: Bonita Nelson, John Benson
Agency Commission: 15%
Manuscript categories represented:
  Nonfiction (self-help, biography, how-to) and fiction (novels).
Agency accepts:
  Telephone Queries: N   Unsolicited Mss: N
          Mail Queries: Y   Poetry Collections: Y

Fees are $325 for manuscripts up to 80,000 words, and $10 per 5,000 words thereafter.

New Age World Services & Books
62091 Valley View Circle
Joshua Tree, CA 92252
Phone: (619) 366-2833

Contact: Victoria E. Vandertuin
Agency Commission: not specified
Manuscript categories represented:
  Specialize in new age fiction and nonfiction. Also represent occult, UFO, metaphysical, lost continents, mystical, ancient astronauts, para-sciences, new age religious, and poetry.

Agency accepts:
  Telephone Queries: Y   Unsolicited Mss: Y
      Mail Queries: Y   Poetry Collections: Y

Charge reading, criticism, and representation fees. Will read at no charge unsolicited queries and outlines with character description and a few pages of sample writing.

New Voices Literary Agency
5907 Main Street
Williamsville, NY 14221
Phone: (716) 626-4370 Fax: (716) 626-4388

Contact: Jason Kelly
Agency Commission: 10%
Manuscript categories represented:
  Fiction (novels, short story collections), nonfiction, screenplays, children's literature. In fiction, specialize in romance, suspense, literary, mainstream, science fiction, adventure; in nonfiction, self-help, professional.
Agency accepts:
  Telephone Queries: Y   Unsolicited Mss: N
      Mail Queries: Y   Poetry Collections: Y

"We charge at the simple rate of $1 per page, which comes to about $300 for a 100,000-word manuscript."

Northeast Literary Agency
69 Broadway
Concord, NH 03301
Phone: (603) 225-9162

Contact: Victor Levine
Agency Commission: 15% U.S., 25% abroad
Manuscript categories represented:
  All; specialize in popular fiction and nonfiction.
Agency accepts:
  Telephone Queries: Y   Unsolicited Mss: Y
        Mail Queries: Y   Poetry Collections: Y

Evaluation fee for 50 pages or less is $95; for full-length manuscripts, $250.

Evelyn Oppenheimer
7929 Meadow Park Drive, #201
Dallas, TX 75230
Phone: (214) 369-2448

Contact: Evelyn Oppenheimer
Agency Commission: 15%
Manuscript categories represented:
  Adult book-length fiction and nonfiction.
Agency accepts:
  Telephone Queries: Y   Unsolicited Mss: N
        Mail Queries: Y   Poetry Collections: N

Always query first; response to query will describe fee structure.

Pegasus International, Inc.
P.O. Box 5470
Winter Park, FL 32793-5470
Phone: (407) 831-1008

Contact: Carole Morling
Agency Commission: 10% U.S., 15% abroad
Manuscript categories represented:
Novels: mainstream, horror, science fiction, new age, romance. Nonfiction: top-level material in all genres. Particularly interested in helping unpublished authors; prefer working by phone.
Agency accepts:

Telephone Queries: Y	Unsolicited Mss: Y
Mail Queries: Y	Poetry Collections: Y

One-time reading fee reimbursed upon publication: $200 for up to a 400-page double-spaced manuscript. Lower fees for chapbooks, etc. We pay all postage/phone calls; no hidden fees.

Perkins Literary Agency
P.O. Box 48
Childs, MD 21916-0048
Phone: (301) 398-2647

Contact: Esther R. Perkins
Agency Commission: 15% U.S., 20% abroad
Manuscript categories represented:
Fiction only: specialize in mystery, historical romance, Regency. Also represent male action/adventure and a few contemporary novels.
Agency accepts:

Telephone Queries: N	Unsolicited Mss: N
Mail Queries: Y	Poetry Collections: N

Fee charged to anyone not published by a major publisher within the past two years; this is refunded in full if sale is made within one year.

Raintree Agency
360 West 21st Street
New York, NY 10011
Phone: (212) 242-2387

Contact: Diane Raintree
Agency Commission: 10%
Manuscript categories represented:
    Specialize in children's books, plays, and film scripts.
    Also represent adult novels and television scripts.
Agency accepts:
    Telephone Queries: Y   Unsolicited Mss: N
            Mail Queries: Y   Poetry Collections: N

"All scripts are read by me personally. I talk with the writer before and afterward. The goal is to be sure the work is outstanding before I submit it to a publisher or to a producer."

Rhodes Literary Agency
Box 89133
Honolulu, HI 96830-9133
Phone: (808) 947-4689

Contact: Fred C. Pugarelli
Agency Commission: 15% U.S., 20% abroad
Manuscript categories represented:
    All categories; specialize in novels and film scripts.

Agency accepts:
  Telephone Queries: Y   Unsolicited Mss: N
        Mail Queries: Y   Poetry Collections: Y

$145 for standard-length novels, nonfiction books, screenplays. $155 for overlength novels, nonfiction books, screenplays. $100 for short stories, articles, other short material.

The Allen Ruskin Agency
One Hickory Drive
New City, NY 10956
Phone: (914) 639-9424

Contact: Allen Ruskin
Agency Commission: not specified
Manuscript categories represented:
  Fiction, nonfiction, film and television rights, software.
Agency accepts:
  Telephone Queries: Y   Unsolicited Mss: Y
        Mail Queries: Y   Poetry Collections: N

Fee depends upon length of manuscript.

SLC Enterprises, Inc.
Box 916
Southwest Harbor, ME 04679
Phone: (312) 728-3997 Fax: (207) 244-9933

Contact: Stephen Cogil
Agency Commission: 15%

Manuscript categories represented:

Fiction, poetry, nonfiction. Specialize in sports books.

Agency accepts:

| Telephone Queries: Y | Unsolicited Mss: Y |
| Mail Queries: Y | Poetry Collections: Y |

$150 fee for reading and evaluation of complete manuscript. If book is sold, $150 is deducted from agency commission. Branch office: 852 Highland Place, Highland Park, IL 60035

Southern Writers
Div. of The Habersham Corp.
635 Gravier Street
Suite 1020
New Orleans, LA 70130
Phone: (504) 525-6390 Fax: (504) 524-7349

Contact: Pamela G. Ahearn
Agency Commission: 15% U.S., 20% dramatic and abroad

Manuscript categories represented:

All adult fiction and nonfiction; some young adult. Specialize in historical and contemporary romance, and material relating to the South. No autobiographies, short fiction, articles, or poetry.

Agency accepts:

| Telephone Queries: Y | Unsolicited Mss: N |
| Mail Queries: Y | Poetry Collections: N |

"We charge reading fees to previously unpublished authors, and to authors writing in areas other than those of previous publication. A critique follows, usually 3 to 5 single-spaced pages."

Michael Steinberg, Literary Agent
Box 274
Glencoe, IL 60022
Phone: (708) 835-8881

Contact: Michael Steinberg
Agency Commission: 15%
Manuscript categories represented:
   Specialize in business and finance. Also represent science fiction and mystery.
Agency accepts:
   Telephone Queries: Y   Unsolicited Mss: N
          Mail Queries: Y   Poetry Collections: N

$75 for outline and chapters 1 through 3. $200 for full manuscript to 100,000 words.

Marianne Strong Literary Agency
65 East 96th Street
New York, NY 10128
Phone: (212) 249-1000 Fax: (212) 831-3241

Contact: Marianne Strong
Agency Commission: 15%
Manuscript categories represented:
   Nonfiction: biographies, cookbooks, lifestyle, gossip.
Agency accepts:

Telephone Queries: Y   Unsolicited Mss: N
Mail Queries: Y   Poetry Collections: N

$100 reading fee. $150 for marketing expenses, refundable if book is sold. No charge to paid television and film writers and authors published by a known publisher within the past two years.

Phyllis R. Tornetta
P.O. Box 423
Croton-on-Hudson, NY 10521
Phone: (914) 737-3464

Contact: Phyllis Tornetta
Agency Commission: 15% U.S.
Manuscript categories represented:
  Fiction: romance, contemporary, historical.
Agency accepts:
  Telephone Queries: Y   Unsolicited Mss: N
          Mail Queries: Y   Poetry Collections: N

$100 for full manuscript.

Carlson Wade Literary Agency
49 Bokee Court
Room 4K
Brooklyn, NY 11223
Phone: (718) 743-6983

Contact: Carlson Wade
Agency Commission: 10%

Manuscript categories represented:
  "All categories, short and long."
Agency accepts:
  Telephone Queries: Y   Unsolicited Mss: Y
        Mail Queries: Y   Poetry Collections: N

Books, $50. Short material, $10. "Will give full report and help if needed."

James Warren Literary Agency
13131 Welby Way
Suite A
North Hollywood, CA 91606
Phone: (818) 982-5423

Contact: James Warren
Agency Commission: 15% first sale, 10% thereafter;
  20% abroad
Manuscript categories represented:
  Fiction, nonfiction, children's books.
Agency accepts:
  Telephone Queries: Y   Unsolicited Mss: N
        Mail Queries: Y   Poetry Collections: N

$2.50 per thousand words for authors previously unpublished or published more than five years prior.

Stephen Wright, Authors' Representative
Box 1341, FDR Station
New York, NY 10150
Phone: (212) 213-4382

Contact: Stephen Wright

Agency Commission: 10% for published authors, 15% for unpublished

Manuscript categories represented:

Almost all categories of fiction, nonfiction. "Every submission is individual and different. If any specialty, it's the mystery."

Agency accepts:

Telephone Queries: N	Unsolicited Mss: N
Mail Queries: Y	Poetry Collections: N

Fee depends on the manuscript, e.g., partial or complete.

Tom Zelasky Literary Agency
3138 Parkridge Crescent
Chamblee, GA 30341
Phone: (404) 458-0391

Contact: Tom Zelasky

Agency Commission: 15%

Manuscript categories represented:

Specialize in fiction: Westerns, detective, mainstream. Also represent young adult, science fiction, action, romance, historical.

Agency accepts:

Telephone Queries: Y	Unsolicited Mss: N
Mail Queries: Y	Poetry Collections: N

$100 per 450 pages. Additional fee of $25 for between 450 and 500 pages and per hundred pages above that.

WHERE TO FIND
MORE AGENTS

The reference books listed below can be found in most libraries.

A Guide to Literary Agents and Art/Photo Reps
Writer's Digest Books
1507 Dana Avenue
Cincinnati, OH 45207 (800) 289-0963 outside Ohio;
(513) 531-2222 in Ohio

Annual. $15.95

The 1992 edition lists 500 agencies, both commission and fee-charging.

Information given: name of agency; address; principal contact; commission rate: kinds of work handled.

Further information may include: policy on unsolicited queries and manuscripts; tips on submitting
work to agents and editors; recent sales.

Association of Authors' Representatives (AAR)
10 Astor Place, 3rd floor
New York, NY 10003 (212) 353-3709

A nonprofit membership organization of approximately
250 literary and dramatic agents, the AAR was
formed in 1991 through the merger of the Society of
Authors' Representatives (founded in 1928) and the
Independent Literary Agents Association (founded
in 1977). At regular meetings and seminars, AAR
members discuss important issues concerning writers
and agents. The AAR aims to keep agents informed
about conditions in publishing, the theater, the motion picture and television industries, and related
fields; encourage cooperation among literary organizations; and assist agents in representing their au-
thor-clients' interests.

For $5 (check or money order) plus a #10 self-addressed
envelope stamped with 52¢ postage, the AAR pro-
vides a brochure that outlines its objectives and de-
scribes the author-agent relationship; a listing of its
members with their addresses and phone numbers;
and a copy of its Canon of Ethics.

To qualify for membership, an agent must meet professional standards specified by the organization's by-
laws and agree to subscribe to its Canon of Ethics.

The AAR will accept no new member-agents who charge reading fees, although a few fee-charging members formerly listed with ILAA remain on the list. These agents, designated "RF," must adhere to a carefully controlled procedure that requires them to send writers a detailed, written description of the services offered, total fees, approximate response time, and the qualifications of the individuals reading the work.

Literary Agents of North America
Author Aid/Research Associates International
340 East 52nd Street
New York, NY 10022 (212) 758-4213; 980-9179

$29.95

The 1991 fourth edition lists over 1,000 agents in the United States and Canada.

Information given: name of agency; address; telephone number; contacts; commission rates. Additional information may include: profiles of agency heads; foreign representatives; agency policies; number of clients; manuscript categories; specialties; subject interests; professional listings. Indexed.

Literary Market Place (LMP)
R.R. Bowker Company
245 West 17th Street
New York, NY 10011 Orders: (800) 521-8110

Annual. $134.95

LMP is the "phone book" of the trade publishing industry. It includes a comprehensive listing of book agents: all reputable commission agents and some "mixed" agencies (commission and fee-charging). To be listed, agencies must provide letters of reference from publishers that show the agents to be well established and active in the previous year.

The 1991 edition lists 472 agents.

Information given: name of agency; address; telephone number; principal contact. Further information may include: names of all agents in the firm; names of foreign representatives; specific areas of interest; policies on manuscript submission; membership listing.

Writers Guild of America, East, Inc.
555 West 57th Street
New York, NY 10019 (212) 767-7800

or

Writers Guild of America, West, Inc.
8955 Beverly Boulevard
West Hollywood, California 90048-2456 (310) 550-1000

List of screenplay agents:
WGA, East—$1.08 at the Guild office, $1.37 if mailed in New York State, and $1.29 if mailed out of state. Check or money order only.
WGA, West—free at the Guild office; $1 if mailed.

A comprehensive and reliable list for those who write for radio, television, and film. All agencies on the list have signed the Guild's Artists-Manager Basic Agreement (AMBA). All agree to charge no fee other than a 10% commission on sales.

Information given: name of agency; address; telephone number; whether or not agency handles "material from novice writers."

The Writer's Handbook
The Writer, Inc.
120 Boylston Street
Boston, MA 02116 (617) 423-3157

Annual. $28.95

The 1992 edition lists approximately 100 agencies.

Information given: name of agency; address.

A SELECTED
BIBLIOGRAPHY

Publishers Weekly
Cahners Publishing Co.
249 West 17th Street
New York, NY 10011 Subscriptions and single copy
orders: (800) 842-1669

The trade magazine of the publishing industry. Paul Nathan's "Rights" column reports on outstanding agencies and the prices they get for the sale of various rights. *Publishers Weekly* is available for $119 per year (51 issues); single copies, $5, which includes postage and handling. Most libraries subscribe; consult your library's reference or periodical section.

The Writer
The Writer, Inc.
120 Boylston Street
Boston, MA 02116 (617) 423-3157

Subscription: $27 per year (12 issues)
Single copy: $3; $2 at newsstand
News for writers in all fields, with emphasis on marketing and writing techniques.

Writer's Digest
F & W Publications, Inc.
1507 Dana Avenue
Cincinnati, OH 45207 Subscriptions: (800) 289-0963
outside Ohio; (513) 531-2222
in Ohio

Subscription: $21 per year (12 issues)
Single copy: $3
News for writers in all fields, with emphasis on marketing and writing techniques.

The following publications are available from Poets & Writers, Inc., 72 Spring Street, 3rd floor, New York, NY 10012, (212) 226-3586. Please call or write for an order form.

Poets & Writers Magazine
Essays, interviews, and articles on practical topics of interest for writers. Extensive coverage of grants and awards, deadlines for application, and calls for manuscript submissions. 6 issues a year.

A Directory of American Poets and Fiction Writers, 1993–94 Edition
The names, addresses, and telephone numbers of 6,960 poets and fiction writers who publish in the U.S. Biannual.

A Writer's Guide to Copyright, Second Edition
Completely revised and updated; a clear, concise summary of current copyright law for writers, editors, and teachers.

Author & Audience: A Readings and Workshops Guide
Completely revised and updated; approximately 400 organizations that present readings or workshops in the U.S. An introduction explains how to organize and promote readings and workshops. An essential manual for both presenters and writers.

Literary Bookstores: A Cross-Country Guide
Completely revised and updated; 275 bookstores nationwide that carry contemporary fiction and poetry published by commercial, university, and small presses. Includes an appendix listing literary bars and coffee houses.

Guide to Writers' Conferences
Approximately 150 conferences in the U.S. and abroad; dates, addresses, fees, deadlines, and workshop leaders. Published each March.

ABOUT
POETS & WRITERS

Poets & Writers, Inc., works as a resource for writers, as well as for publishers, schools, and organizations that need to keep in touch with writers. We provide our services through four programs: Publications, the Information Center, Readings/Workshops, and The Writers Exchange.

Publications from Poets & Writers include references, source books, guides, and a magazine published six times a year. For a complete listing, consult the bibliography on pages 188–190.

The Information Center keeps track of current facts about poets and fiction writers active in the U.S. literary community today. A data base includes addresses for 6,960 published American poets and fiction writers. The Information Center staff also answers questions about such practical matters as workshops, conferences, publication, and resources. Telephone information lines are open from 11:00 A.M. to 3:00 P.M. (EST) Monday through Friday.

The Readings/Workshops Program develops audiences for contemporary literature and helps writers survive financially by funding public readings and writing workshops. Community-based organizations are eligible to apply for funding, and poets, fiction writers, essayists, and literary performance artists are welcome to initiate programs with sponsors. For more information, call or write the Readings/Workshops Program at Poets & Writers.

The Writers Exchange is a national program that introduces emerging writers to literary communities outside of their home states. Writers, selected on a competitive basis, meet with a variety of publishers, editors, and well-known authors and share their work through public readings. Only writers from selected states are eligible. For more information, call or write the Writers Exchange at Poets & Writers.

The services and publications of Poets & Writers are supported by a grant from the Literature Program of the National Endowment for the Arts, a federal agency. The Readings/Workshops Program receives major support from the Literature Program of the New York State Council on the Arts and The Lila Wallace-Reader's Digest Fund. Poets & Writers also receives contributions from corporations, foundations, and generous individual donors.

Poets & Writers, Inc., is located at 72 Spring Street, New York, NY 10012; telephone (212) 226-3586, Fax (212) 226-3963.

FOR THE BEST IN PAPERBACKS, LOOK FOR THE

In every corner of the world, on every subject under the sun, Penguin represents quality and variety—the very best in publishing today.

For complete information about books available from Penguin—including Puffins, Penguin Classics, and Arkana—and how to order them, write to us at the appropriate address below. Please note that for copyright reasons the selection of books varies from country to country.

In the United Kingdom: Please write to *Dept. JC, Penguin Books Ltd, FREEPOST, West Drayton, Middlesex UB7 0BR*.

If you have any difficulty in obtaining a title, please send your order with the correct money, plus ten percent for postage and packaging, to *P.O. Box No. 11, West Drayton, Middlesex UB7 0BR*

In the United States: Please write to *Consumer Sales, Penguin USA, P.O. Box 999, Dept. 17109, Bergenfield, New Jersey 07621-0120.* VISA and MasterCard holders call 1-800-253-6476 to order all Penguin titles

In Canada: Please write to *Penguin Books Canada Ltd, 10 Alcorn Avenue, Suite 300, Toronto, Ontario M4V 3B2*

In Australia: Please write to *Penguin Books Australia Ltd, P.O. Box 257, Ringwood, Victoria 3134*

In New Zealand: Please write to *Penguin Books (NZ) Ltd, Private Bag 102902, North Shore Mail Centre, Auckland 10*

In India: Please write to *Penguin Books India Pvt Ltd, 706 Eros Apartments, 56 Nehru Place, New Delhi 110 019*

In the Netherlands: Please write to *Penguin Books Netherlands bv, Postbus 3507, NL-1001 AH Amsterdam*

In Germany: Please write to *Penguin Books Deutschland GmbH, Metzlerstrasse 26, 60594 Frankfurt am Main*

In Spain: Please write to *Penguin Books S. A., Bravo Murillo 19, 1° B, 28015 Madrid*

In Italy: Please write to *Penguin Italia s.r.l., Via Felice Casati 20, I-20124 Milano*

In France: Please write to *Penguin France S. A., 17 rue Lejeune, F–31000 Toulouse*

In Japan: Please write to *Penguin Books Japan, Ishikiribashi Building, 2–5–4, Suido, Bunkyo-ku, Tokyo 112*

In Greece: Please write to *Penguin Hellas Ltd, Dimocritou 3, GR–106 71 Athens*

In South Africa: Please write to *Longman Penguin Southern Africa (Pty) Ltd, Private Bag X08, Bertsham 2013*